Socrates Meets Descartes

Other Works of Peter Kreeft from St. Augustine's Press

Philosophy 101 by Socrates
Socrates Meets Freud
Socrates Meets Hume
Socrates Meets Kant
Socrates Meets Kierkegaard
Socrates Meets Machiavelli
Socrates Meets Marx
Socrates Meets Sartre
The Philosophy of Jesus (also in audio format)
Jesus-Shock (also in audio format)
Summa Philosophica
Socratic Logic
Socrates' Children: Ancient
Socrates' Children: Medieval
Socrates' Children: Modern
Socrates' Children: Contemporary
Socrates' Children [all four books in one]
An Ocean Full of Angels
The Sea Within
I Surf, Therefore I Am
If Einstein Had Been a Surfer

Socrates Meets Descartes

The Father of Philosophy Analyzes the Father of Modern Philosophy's *Discourse on Method*

By Peter Kreeft

St. Augustine's Press
South Bend, Indiana

For Joseph Flanagan, S.J.

Contents

Preface 9
Introduction 11

1. The Meeting 17
2. The Main Point 23
3. The Beginning 30
4. Is Philosophy a Science? 43
5. Descartes' Hidden Agenda 61
6. Knowledge's Goal 71
7. The Search for Certainty 77
8. The Reason for the New Method 98
9. Who Can Use the New Method? 108
10. The Method Itself 114
11. Descartes' Mathematicism 133
12. Descartes' Provisional Morality 138
13. Step One of Descartes' Philosophical
    System: Universal Doubt 143
14. Step Two of Descartes' Philosophical
    System: "I Think, Therefore I Am" 157
15. Step Three of Descartes' Philosophical
    System: "*What* I Am" (Descartes'
    Anthropology) 170
16. Step Four of Descartes' Philosophical
    System: The Criterion of Truth 184
17. Step Five of Descartes' Philosophical
    System: Proofs for God's Existence 191

7

18. Step Six of Descartes' Philosophical
    System: The Proof of the Existence of
    the Material World 209
19. Descartes and the Future of Mankind 219
20. Descartes' Legacy 234

Preface

This book is one in a series of Socratic explorations of some of the Great Books. Books in this series are intended to be short, clear, and non-technical, thus fully understandable by beginners. They also introduce (or review) the basic questions in the fundamental divisions of philosophy (see the chapter titles): metaphysics, epistemology, anthropology, ethics, logic, and method. They are designed both for classroom use and for educational do-it-yourselfers. The "Socrates Meets . . ." books can be read and understood completely on their own, but each is best appreciated after reading the little classic it engages in dialogue.

The setting—Socrates and the author of the Great Book meeting in the afterlife—need not deter readers who do not believe there is an afterlife. For although the two characters and their philosophies are historically real, their conversation, of course, is not and requires a "willing suspension of disbelief". There is no reason the skeptic cannot extend this literary belief also to the setting.

Introduction

Socrates and Descartes are probably the two most important philosophers who ever lived, because they are the two who made the most difference to all philosophy after them. Socrates is often called "the Father of Philosophy" and Descartes is called "the Father of Modern Philosophy." The two of them stand at the beginning of the two basic philosophical options: the classical and the modern.

At least seven features unite these two philosophers and distinguish them from all others.

First, each was an initiator, a revolutionary, virtually without predecessors. No other philosophers depended so little on previous philosophers, and no other philosophers made subsequent thinkers depend so much on them. Socrates' method, Socrates' questions, and Socrates' answers differed almost totally from the so-called pre-Socratic philosophers; and Descartes tried to begin philosophy all over again as if the two thousand years of it before him simply had not existed. No one else in the history of thought has ever done this as thoroughly as these two did.

Second, each began by doubting and questioning everything, or nearly everything, even the commonplaces everyone else took for granted. Both understood that the first and most important step of a truly scientific method is to assume nothing, or at least to question all assumptions, to get prejudices out, out from the subjective side of consciousness and into the

objective side, where they can be part of the exami-
nees rather than part of the examiners.

Many other philosophers agree with this, of course,
but none ever did it more thoroughly or originally
than these two. Socrates had few books, no schools,
and little philosophical tradition before him to work
with; Descartes had much, but deliberately doubted
it all (or tried to). Thus both relied on the direct experience and thinking of the individual, not the authority and tradition of the community.

Third, each made the quest for the knowledge of
the self the central philosophical quest, though they
meant somewhat different things by it. What Socrates
meant by "know thyself" was "know Man's essence,
know universal human nature." What Descartes
meant was "know your own existence as an individual."

They also undertook this quest for different reasons. Socrates' reason was obedience to the command
of the god of the Delphic oracle, over whose tem-
ple "know thyself" was inscribed. Descartes' reason
was to overcome the skepticism of many of the best
thinkers of his time (especially Montaigne) by discovering the one absolute certainty that could be used as
the starting point of a new, more certain philosophy:
"I think, therefore I am." But both men turned to the
"I", the self, the soul, the mind, as their fundamental
interest, much more than any other philosophers had.
(Descartes' only rivals here are Augustine, twelve
centuries before him, and Pascal, his contemporary;
Socrates had no other preceding or contemporary rivals at all.)

Fourth, each identified the self with the soul rather

than the body. Each was a "dualist"; that is, they believed that reality is dual (twofold): matter (including our bodies) and spirit (including our souls). No philosophers were more famous dualists than Descartes and Socrates (via his disciple Plato).

Fifth, each focused on the epistemological question, or "the critical problem" of How do you know? Socrates asked this question about every particular claim anyone made to know anything, while Descartes asked it about knowledge in general. Unlike Socrates, Descartes demanded a reason for trusting reason itself before using reason to construct a philosophy, as a carpenter might check his tools before building a house. Perhaps this is an answerable question, perhaps not. But in any case, no two philosophers ever focused more attention on the question How do you know? than these two.

Sixth, each offered a new method to philosophy, though both came to traditional conclusions through their new methods. In both cases, the new method demanded more severe criteria, tighter, stricter grounds for our beliefs and opinions. Each philosopher narrowed "reason". Before Socrates, it had included myth, intuition, and tradition. Without rejecting any of these older things, Socrates demanded something new: clear definitions and logical arguments. Descartes narrowed "reason" further, from "wisdom" to "science", from philosophical logic to scientific logic, from Socrates' "dialectical" (dialogue) method to the scientific method. No other philosophers ever offered new methods that changed philosophical thinking itself as much as these two. And no philosopher's method ever proved more popular, more universally imitated by his successors, than these two.

Seventh, each believed he was divinely commissioned to philosophize by a supernatural sign. For Socrates, it was the Delphic oracle, who, by announcing to Socrates' friend Chairophon that no one was wiser than Socrates, inveigled Socrates to question others to find someone wiser than himself, and in so doing inveigled Socrates to develop the Socratic Method of philosophizing by logical cross-examination.

Socrates also confessed that he had a private "spiritual sign" or "divine voice", which often stopped him from some course of action but never specifically commanded any. Like most idealistic Athenian citizens of his time, Socrates had aspired to a political career, but the "divine voice" forbade him. So together, the Delphic oracle and the "divine voice" led him into philosophy. In his *Apology*, he defends not only himself but his troublemaking vocation of philosophizing; and every single time he mentions philosophy in that speech, he mentions "the god" as the source of his vocation to philosophize.

Descartes, too, became a philosopher due to an apparent divine intervention. Already at age twenty-three he was clearly a scientific genius, and he delayed publishing only because of the condemnation of Galileo. On the night of November 10, 1619, he had a life-changing dream in which he believed that the divine Spirit of Truth came to him and directed him to philosophize.

I need not add that this is not how most philosophers and philosophies begin. Socrates and Descartes are strikingly unusual and strikingly similar in these seven different ways. Yet they are also strikingly different from each other, as different as the ancient (classical) and modern (scientific) worldviews of which they were major founders.

So a dialogue between Socrates and Descartes is a dialogue between the two fundamental stages in the history of philosophy, the history of consciousness, and the history of Western culture.

I

The Meeting

DESCARTES: I must be dreaming. I thought I was dying, but now I seem to be very much alive. I know I was middle-aged and ill, but now I feel young and healthy. I thought I was in a cold bed in the damp, dark winter land of Sweden, and now I seem to be riding this magnificent white horse down this sunny road in a beautiful land that looks like the south of France.

And there is someone ahead, waving for me to stop. Is it an angel? Oh, no; no angel could look like *that*. It looks like a pig—it looks like a frog—it looks like Socrates—by Jove, it seems to *be* Socrates!

SOCRATES: Right the third time, René. "Third time's the charm", as we used to say back in Greece.

DESCARTES: Are you—an angel?

SOCRATES: Hardly!

DESCARTES: Is this—Heaven?

SOCRATES: Not yet. But this is the road.

DESCARTES: Were you sent to meet me—by Higher Authorities?

SOCRATES: I was.

DESCARTES: So I *am* dead. Or, rather, my body is.

SOCRATES: Your old body, anyway.

DESCARTES: Then what is riding this horse? I have a right to know!

SOCRATES: My Higher Authorities do not allow me to answer questions about that now.

DESCARTES: What would your Higher Authorities have me to do?

SOCRATES: Get down off your high horse.

DESCARTES: Oh. All right. There! It's done. What next? Will you lead me to Heaven?

SOCRATES: I must send your horse to Heaven first. There, off you go!

DESCARTES: He seems to know the way; look at him fly! But why must I wait? Why does my horse go to Heaven before me?

SOCRATES: Because we make no mistakes here. And everyone knows that it is a mistake to put Descartes before the horse.

DESCARTES: You may make no mistakes here but you certainly make terrible puns. And why are we speaking English, not French or Greek?

SOCRATES: Because that is the language of the man who is writing this book that we are in.

DESCARTES: Oh. I hope he does not have an addiction to puns. A pun is the lowest form of humor, don't you know? A kind of literary disease. Is that his pitiful idea of a joke?

SOCRATES: No, it is His.

DESCARTES: Whose?

SOCRATES: The Author of the author of the book we are in. The Creator.

DESCARTES: Oh. Perhaps my sense of humor needs to get down off its high horse. Apparently the transcendent Creator stoops to rather low depths of humor.

SOCRATES: Oh, He has stooped to far lower depths than that.

DESCARTES: Is He a comedian, then?

SOCRATES: But of course!

DESCARTES: Excuse me for being surprised and even a bit skeptical. That pun was not the mark of a great comedian. It did not seem to have the style and grace of . . .

SOCRATES: Of a French aristocrat? No. Does it surprise you to learn that God is not a French aristocrat?

DESCARTES: Well, no. But the *Creator* . . .

SOCRATES: And have you ever carefully observed His creations? Have you ever gazed into the face of an ostrich? Or observed the play of meerkats? Or, for that matter, of French aristocrats?

DESCARTES: Touché, Socrates. You *are* the real Socrates, aren't you?

SOCRATES: As much as you are the real Descartes.

DESCARTES: Are you playing with me?

SOCRATES: No, I am testing you. Do you doubt your own existence?

DESCARTES: No.

SOCRATES: Then do not doubt mine either.

DESCARTES: Actually, I *did* doubt my own existence, and everything else as well. Universal doubt was the first step of the method I taught.

SOCRATES: So you do not practice what you preach?

DESCARTES: No, no, I did not preach skepticism. Skepticism means doubting all things at all times. My method was my *answer* to skepticism. Once we pass through universal doubt, we may rightly claim certain knowledge of any idea that proves indubitable —first of all, the idea of our own existence.

SOCRATES: I think I see an analogy here. Your universal doubt functions rather like death; and the idea of your own existence is rather like the soul, and its indubitability is rather like the soul's immortality, and the certain knowledge thus attained is rather like Heaven's Beatific Vision, and passing through your philosophical method is rather like a resurrection. Is this not so?

DESCARTES: That sounds a bit . . . a bit much! I never quite thought of it that way.

SOCRATES: How *did* you think of it?

DESCARTES: Simply as a way to overcome debilitating skepticism so as to lay a foundation for the sciences. As I explained in my *Discourse on Method* . . .

SOCRATES: This book, you mean?

DESCARTES: Is it here?

SOCRATES: See for yourself.

DESCARTES: Then—there are books in Heaven?

SOCRATES: Did I say this was Heaven? I thought you made no assumptions. Isn't that the very first step of your method?

DESCARTES: I never recommended the practice of my method in daily life. In fact . . . perhaps I have a riddle for you, Socrates. How does Descartes differ from the Blessed Virgin?

SOCRATES: Tell me.

DESCARTES: She made only one Assumption.

SOCRATES: If punning is "the literary disease", this disease seems to be infectious.

DESCARTES: So this is not Heaven?

SOCRATES: Not yet. Not for you, at least.

DESCARTES: Not for me—as distinct from my horse?

SOCRATES: As distinguished from me. This is Heaven for me but Purgatory for you. For you must endure my cross-examination of your book.

DESCARTES: Oh, that is a far, far pleasanter Purgatory than I had ever dared to hope for. Examine away, then, Socrates. I have had many delightful conversations and correspondences on earth in pursuit of the truth, but this is a far, far better thing I do than ever I have done.

SOCRATES: And if you are in pursuit of the truth, you shall go to a far, far better place than ever you have been.

2

The Main Point

SOCRATES: Before we explore and evaluate your book, we should understand your reason for writing it. What need did it address? It must have been a great need, because it had a great success, for many centuries after your death. It was one of the most thought-changing books ever written.

DESCARTES: So you can see the future here?

SOCRATES: It is not "future" here. All is present.

DESCARTES: You know everything, then?

SOCRATES: Of course not.

DESCARTES: How much, then?

SOCRATES: As much as we need to.

DESCARTES: But not as much as you want to?

SOCRATES: Not so. That is the difference between this world and the old one: gaps are gone, the gap between present and future and also the gap between wants and needs.

DESCARTES: That must be the secret of your happiness, then, as Marcus Aurelius taught. Say, is he here?

SOCRATES: There will be plenty of time later for such questions.

DESCARTES: But I have a good memory, and I remember you saying that in this place the gap is gone —the gap between wants and needs. And I *want* to know about Marcus Aurelius.

SOCRATES: You do *not* have a good memory. For you do not remember my saying that this is only Heaven for me. For you it is Purgatory.

DESCARTES: Oh. What must I do . . . ?

SOCRATES: For now, you must help me to explore the questions in your book rather than the questions in your mind about this world.

DESCARTES: Why are *you* sent to me?

SOCRATES: Because your book revolutionized philosophy, and that was the enterprise I had the good fortune to begin, or rather to be used as a divine instrument to help others to begin. So please begin by telling me what need you saw in your world and how you tried to supply that need in your book.

DESCARTES: Gladly. I think I can summarize that in two images: the decline of philosophy and the rise of all the other sciences.

When I surveyed the philosophical scene, I saw only three options, none of them healthy ones with a future. First, there were the late medieval Scholastic philosophers, obsessively disputing about purely verbal differences, mindlessly mouthing traditional formulas, endlessly multiplying hair-splitting distinctions, and treating abstractions as the only realities. Second, there were the nature mystics, the occultists and alchemists and astrologers. I thought of both these and the Scholastics as comic figures. Serious philosophical minds were becoming skeptics, like Montaigne. And that was the third option, skepticism. I wanted to offer a radical alternative to all three, beginning with a refutation of skepticism and proceeding to a philosophy that was truly scientific.

SOCRATES: What did you mean by "scientific"?

DESCARTES: That is indeed a key concept. While philosophy was languishing in the doldrums, every one of the sciences had been making remarkable progress. In fact, there had been more progress in the sciences in one century than in all previous centuries combined. So I asked myself the obvious question, why? Why this tremendous progress in all sciences except philosophy? And my answer, in one word, was: method. The scientific method was the greatest discovery in the history of science, because it was the skeleton key that opened all the doors in all the sciences. Every one, that is, except one: philosophy. That is why I decided to write *Discourse on Method*. It was an experiment to test the hypothesis that this method could revitalize philosophy as well.

SOCRATES: Your experiment sounds most reasonable. You understand the assumption behind it, of course?

DESCARTES: I made no assumptions. It was an *experiment*; I did not assume any particular result beforehand.

SOCRATES: But you assumed that philosophy is a science, in assuming that it could use the scientific method, did you not?

DESCARTES: Oh, of course—that it is a science in the generic sense: an organized body of knowledge, explaining things through causes and proving truths through rational demonstrations. I know it is not like the other sciences in that it does not have some particular field of data. But it takes as its field all fields, and it does not confine itself to sensation for its data. In that way it is like mathematics; but it does not use quantitative measurement as mathematics does. But I hoped to find the very essence of the scientific method that was common to the empirical sciences and the mathematical sciences—*and* the philosophical sciences. If I could find that, and define it, and summarize its basic rules, then I would supply what was needed: the single essential method that could be applied to philosophy just as effectively as it had been applied to the other sciences.

That is why the most important word in my title, *Discours de la methode*, is the word that was omitted in the English translation *Discourse on Method*: the word "the". This *one* method transformed *all* the sciences, and so I hoped it could also transform philosophy.

SOCRATES: Your hope seems quite understandable. But surely you realized how revolutionary and radical this idea was? For you had a very extensive education in the history of philosophy, and you surely had learned there that Aristotle, the most influential philosopher in the world (and the most commonsensical) had taught that each science required a different method because method is relative to subject matter and each science dealt with different subject matter.

DESCARTES: Of course. But since Aristotle had proved to be wrong in many other points in the sciences, I thought it likely that he had been wrong about method too. Or, at least, that he had missed something. Of course methods in the sciences must vary by subject matter, but is there not something common to all these somewhat different methods that lets us call them all *scientific* methods? And if I could isolate this common essence and formulate its basic principles, I would do for scientific method what Aristotle did for the principles of logic. I would abstract the common from the specific, the general from the particular.

SOCRATES: Isn't that really what *all* rational thinking does?

DESCARTES: Yes, but my point was not just theoretical —to find the most general principles of the method that had already been used so successfully in the sciences—but it was practical: having found and formulated these most general principles, I wanted to apply them to philosophy as no one had ever done before and thus to enable philosophy to do what it had never done before while all the other sciences were doing it: namely, to decide issues definitively, to resolve controversial questions with finality, to arrive at certain answers that end all reasonable doubts, and thus to end the sad divisions between the different schools of thought.

You see, philosophers in my time were still divided over the very same issues that had divided them in the past, in your time in Greece and later in Rome and again in medieval Christendom. But scientists were no longer so divided. They had learned how to settle the issues they had always argued about in the past, because they had discovered this wonderful tool for ending disagreements: the scientific method. So I hoped that if I could use that tool in philosophy I would get the same results there. And this would be even more important, as philosophy is more important than the other sciences and deals with the most important of all questions. But in order to use the tool, I had to first isolate it and define it. That is the purpose of my book.

SOCRATES: You have made the single purpose of your book admirably clear. Can you next explain its division into six subplots, its six parts?

DESCARTES: Yes. This is how I summarized them in my preface: **"In the first, one will find various discussions concerning the sciences."** Here, I explain how I came to discover the method. I give the reader a little autobiography.

DM,
Intro.

   "In the second part, [are] the chief rules of the method which the author has been seeking." The search is explained in Part One, the treasure I found is explained in Part Two.

   "In the third part, [are] some of the rules of morality which the author has derived from this method." This is my first application of the method, to morality, in a very preliminary and temporary way.

   "In the fourth part, [are] the reasons by which the author proves the existence of God and of the human soul, which are the foundations of

metaphysics." This is my second application of the method: to philosophy and philosophical theology. I later expanded this short chapter into an entire book, the *Meditations*.

"In the fifth part . . . [are] **questions in physics which the author has sought. . . ."** This is my third application of the method: to the physical sciences, especially medicine—again, in a very preliminary way.

"And in the final part, what things the author believes are required to advance further in the study of nature." This is my prognosis, or prediction, or prophecy of how much can be accomplished in the future by this marvelous tool.

SOCRATES: How perfectly clear and orderly it sounds! So let us begin our exploration of this extraordinary book.

DESCARTES: Where do you want to begin?

SOCRATES: Why, at the beginning, of course.

3

The Beginning

SOCRATES: We old Greeks had a proverb: "Well be-gun is half done." The point of the proverb is that the most crucial part of any enterprise is the beginning. Old Archimedes said, "Give me a lever long enough and a point to rest it on, and I can move the world." So we must first look carefully at your "Archimedean point", the point on which you rest all the rest of what you say.

DESCARTES: There is indeed such a point, Socrates. That point is, in a sense, the whole "point" of my philosophy: a new foundation, a solid certainty on which to rest all subsequent thinking. And this is my *cogito ergo sum*, "I think, therefore I am." That is the first point of my philosophical system. But it is not until Part Four of my *Discourse on Method* that I sum-marize my philosophical system.

SOCRATES: So there is an even earlier starting point, or "Archimedean point", or beginning.

DESCARTES: Yes.

SOCRATES: And if your book reflects your thought, we will find this beginning of your thought at the beginning of your book, will we not?

DESCARTES: That follows.

SOCRATES: So we need to look very carefully at your very first paragraph.

DESCARTES: Yes. Because that is about reason, the tool with which we do all our thinking, in philosophy and in the other sciences. I believe that we must first examine our tools before we use them to build our buildings. This is as true of mental work as it is of physical work.

But how will we get another copy of my book so we can both be reading it at the same time? Where did you get that copy that you have in your hand? Oh—another copy just appeared in my hand as soon as I conceived the thought of it and the desire for it! Is that how things happen here?

SOCRATES: No, not all things. Just the things that need to happen that way.

DESCARTES: I am curious . . .

SOCRATES: Yes, you are. We accept your confession. And here is your penance: you must now concentrate on the matter at hand, your old book, not your new world.

DESCARTES: Is there not enough time?

SOCRATES: There is enough time for everything here. But we measure time by present moments here, and we measure those moments not by the movement of material bodies like sun and moon but by assigned purposes. This moment is the "now" that is assigned to you. This "now" is the time to investigate your book, not to indulge your curiosity.

DESCARTES: I accept your penance. Let us investigate my first sentence then.

DM 1,
para. 1

SOCRATES: Here it is: **"Good sense is the most evenly divided commodity in the world."** Here is your Archimedean point: that good sense is equal. Is that right?

DESCARTES: Yes. And this is indeed a new "point of departure" in philosophy rather as democracy is in politics, in that it equalizes what was formerly thought to be unequal and hierarchical—a thing possessed more by the few than by the many. So this is a new beginning, a new root or *radix*, and thus truly "radical".

SOCRATES: And that thing which your new starting point declares equal—you call that "good sense"?

DESCARTES: Yes.

SOCRATES: And what do you mean by "good sense"?

DESCARTES: I offer a number of equivalent expressions for it. One could simply be "common sense," for I declare this "good sense" to be common to all men. Another synonym comes two sentences later: **"the power of judging rightly and of distinguishing the true from the false"**. And, in the same sentence, I offer still another synonym, **"reason"**.

DM 1,
para. 1

SOCRATES: Admirably clear! So your very first statement, which is the root or *radix* or "Archimedean point" or beginning of your whole new philosophy, is that *reason is equal in all men.*

DESCARTES: Yes. I democratized reason.

SOCRATES: No beginning should go unquestioned, don't you agree?

DESCARTES: I do.

SOCRATES: And certainly not such a radical new beginning as this one.

DESCARTES: Indeed.

SOCRATES: So we must examine your reasons for believing this new beginning to be true.

DESCARTES: You can find that in the rest of my first paragraph.

SOCRATES: Let us examine this paragraph with the greatest care, then. For it is the fulcrum on which the whole lever of modern philosophy rests. With it we can "leverage" all the rest. It is the beginning of the beginning of the beginning. For modern philosophy begins anew with you, who have been named "the father of modern philosophy"; and you begin with this book; and this book begins with this paragraph.

So tell me how you justify this new beginning.

DESCARTES: I presented this new beginning in three clear steps. (1) First, I stated my basic claim, that reason is equal in all men. (2) Next, I gave a reason for believing this. (3) Finally, I drew the consequence or corollary from it. Those are the three points I made in my first paragraph.

SOCRATES: Would you read it, please?

DESCARTES: (1) **Good sense is the most evenly distributed commodity in the world,** (2) **for each of**   DM 1, para. 1

us considers himself to be so well endowed there-
with that even those who are the most difficult
to please in all other matters are not wont to desire more of it than they have. It is not likely
that anyone is mistaken about this fact. Rather,
it provides evidence that the power of judging
rightly and of distinguishing the true from the
false (which, properly speaking, is what people
call good sense or reason) is naturally equal in
all men. (3) Thus the diversity of our opinions
does not arise from the fact that some people are
more reasonable than others, but simply from the
fact that we conduct our thoughts along different
lines and do not consider the same things. For
it is not enough to have a good mind; the main
thing is to use it well. The greatest souls are capable of the greatest vices as well as of the greatest virtues. And if they always follow the correct
path, those who move forward only very slowly
can make much greater progress than do those
who run and stray from it.

(Le bon sens est la chose du monde la mieux
partagée: car chacun pense en être si bien pourvu,
que ceux même qui sont les plus difficiles à con-
tenter en toute autre chose n'ont point coutume
d'en désirer plus qu'ils en ont. En quoi il n'est pas
vraisemblable que tous se trompent; mais plutôt
cela témoigne que la puissance de bien juger et
distinguer le vrai d'avec le faux, qui est proprement ce qu'on nomme le bon sens ou la raison,
est naturellement égale en tous les hommes; et
ainsi que la diversité de nos opinions ne vient

pas de ce que les uns sont plus raisonnables que les autres, mais seulement de ce que nous conduisons nos pensées par diverses voies, et ne considérons pas les mêmes choses. Car ce n'est pas assez d'avoir l'esprit bon, mais le principal est de l'appliquer bien. Les plus grandes âmes sont capables des plus grands vices aussi bien que des plus grandes vertus, et ceux qui ne marchent que fort lentement peuvent avancer beaucoup davantage, s'ils suivent toujours le droit chemin, que ne font ceux qui courent et qui s'en éloignent.)

SOCRATES: Of these three points of yours, (1) your claim about reason, (2) the premises from which you deduce that claim, and (3) the corollary you deduce from it, which of the three is to you the most important?

DESCARTES: The corollary, surely. For if diversity of opinions stems not from innate differences in reason but only from using different methods, then the use of one method, "*the*" method, would for the first time in history enable mankind to overcome the entrenched differences of opinion and belief that have caused wars, especially religious wars, at all times and places. No one thought this possible until now. The disease is now curable because its cause has now been correctly diagnosed.

SOCRATES: I see. The use of your method could have world-changing consequences.

DESCARTES: Indeed. Of course, I did not dare clearly to claim that in print. In my day, the powers that be always feared radical change, even change for the better.

SOCRATES: You claim that differences of opinion do *not* arise from innate differences in reason, which could never be changed or overcome, but only from differences in method, which *could* be changed—is that correct? Is that all we need to do, use the same method?

DESCARTES: I mention *two* aspects of the scientific method: "the fact that we conduct our thoughts along different lines (*voies*)"—by which I mean, essentially, different *methods*—and the fact that we "do not consider (*considerons*) the same things"—essentially, different *data*. But we can share our data, as good scientists do; and we can all agree to use the same method, as good scientists do—*the* method, the scientific method. And if we do those two things, we will overcome the two sources of disagreement and all be led eventually to the same truth. We cannot share or exchange innate differences, so if reason is innately different in different people, there is no hope for agreement. But if and only if reason is equal in all, can we hope that we will finally reach the kind of worldwide agreement in philosophy that we have reached in the other sciences.

SOCRATES: I am impressed—with the simplicity and clarity and obviousness of your idea and also with its size and power, so to speak, the world-shaking differences it could make.

DESCARTES: Thank you, Socrates. I am deeply gratified by your approval, for I had always thought of myself as your disciple and admirer, and now I find you reciprocating my admiration! I knew I could count on you as an ally in the war against irrationality.

SOCRATES: Be not so hasty, René. I said I was impressed by the simplicity of your idea and with its power. But I did not yet speak of its truth.

DESCARTES: Do you say it is false?

SOCRATES: I do not. How could I know that before I investigate it?

DESCARTES: Oh. Of course. Well, let us investigate, then. We're here to investigate my whole book, aren't we?

SOCRATES: Yes, but one point at a time. And first things first. So let us investigate your very first point, your "Archimedean point" about reason being equal in all: Is this true or is it not?

You give two arguments for its truth. Here is the first one:

> **Good sense is the most evenly divided commodity in the world, *for* each of us considers himself to be so well endowed therewith that even those who are the most difficult to please in all other matters are not wont to desire more of it than they want. [And] it is not likely that anyone is mistaken about this fact. Rather, it provides evidence that . . . reason is naturally equal in all men.**

DM 1, para. 1

May I set your argument out in syllogistic form?

DESCARTES: Be my guest. You invented the syllogism, after all!

SOCRATES: Your conclusion is that reason is equal in all men.
Your expressed premise is that all men *believe* they have enough of it.
Do you see what implied premise you must assume in order to prove this conclusion?

DESCARTES: Of course: that what all men by nature believe, is true.

SOCRATES: Well, then, why is *that* assumption true?

DESCARTES: Because human reason is to be trusted. It is precisely because all men have an equal amount of reason, that we may trust them when they all agree about something. Surely you see the consistency there.

SOCRATES: Ah, but I would call it circularity rather than consistency. You argue that all men *are* equally wise, or reasonable, because they *believe* they are; and you also argue that this *belief* of theirs—that they are wise—is to be trusted because they *are* equally wise. This seems to be a circular argument right at the beginning: a circular argument for your beginning, for your "Archimedean point". This does not look like a very auspicious beginning for a new philosophy that seeks to be more critical and scientific than any one before it!

DESCARTES: Oh, Socrates, I am not that ignorant of logic! You misunderstand my purpose in this sentence, this first reason for my "Archimedean point": it was not meant to be a *proof*, a demonstrative argument. I put it forth only as a *clue*. The reasoning is not what Aristotle and the Scholastic logicians call a "perfect demonstration", from cause to effect, but it moves from effect to cause, from fingerprint to finger. It points, it indicates, it directs your attention back to its cause. If my initial claim is true—that reason is equal—then it would have certain effects, and one of the effects would be that all men would be instinctively satisfied with the amount of reason they have, just as they are instinctively satisfied with the amount of eyes or ears that they have.

SOCRATES: I see your logic now. But not your psychology.

DESCARTES: What do you mean?

SOCRATES: You say that all men are satisfied with the amount of reason they have. I find it remarkable that you take self-satisfaction as a sign of *wisdom*. You who think of yourself as my disciple! I took self-satisfaction to be a sign of folly. That was how I interpreted the puzzle of the Delphic oracle: that no one in the world was wiser than I. It was because of my *dissatisfaction* with my amount of wisdom—an amount I took to be zero—that I was wiser than those others who, having the same amount as I, were nevertheless satisfied with it. And now you assume that those others are all right and wise, rather than wrong and foolish.

DESCARTES: How do I claim that?

SOCRATES: When you say, "It is not likely that anyone is mistaken about this fact."

DESCARTES: Oh.

SOCRATES: And here is what seems to be another irony. No, more than an irony, a paradox. No, more than a paradox, a self-contradiction.

DESCARTES: I thought I was careful always to be logical and avoid self-contradictions. What is it?

SOCRATES: You were probably the single most intelligent man in the world in your time, were you not?

DESCARTES: Since it seems that false modesty cannot trump honesty in this place, I must admit that this is so.

SOCRATES: And were you not the first one to create this new philosophy?

DESCARTES: Yes.

SOCRATES: And is not this philosophy based on the premises in your very first paragraph?

DESCARTES: Yes.

SOCRATES: And is not one of those premises that no man is more or less intelligent than any other?

DESCARTES: Oh.

SOCRATES: Your brilliant, new philosophy—a philosophy no one before you ever created—rests on the premise that no man is any more brilliant than any other.

DESCARTES: Perhaps it takes brilliance to make the discovery that brilliance is common to all men. I democratized reason, and this was radically new.

SOCRATES: What about the men of the past, then? In your democratizing of reason, why did you ignore the democracy of the dead?

DESCARTES: The democracy of the dead?

SOCRATES: Tradition. If you want to extend the franchise to all men, why do you exclude the dead, who are the vast majority of men?

DESCARTES: I was indeed a progressive rather than a conservative, but that is not a self-contradiction, even if it is a mistake. Why do you take that to be a self-contradiction?

SOCRATES: Because you begin by redefining reason as equal in all men, but your egalitarian redefinition of reason is an act of elitism! For most men disagree with it.

DESCARTES: That sounds very clever, Socrates. But my reply to it is very simple.

SOCRATES: I'm waiting.

DESCARTES: I do not contradict myself here because I do *not* claim to be an elitist, or wiser than anyone else. In fact, I write:

For myself, I have never presumed that my mind was in any respect more perfect than anyone else's. In fact, I have often longed to have as quick a wit or as precise and distinct an imagination or as full and responsive a memory as certain other people.

DM 1,
para. 2

SOCRATES: Oh, but there you go again, contradicting yourself! For you now say your mind is *inferior* to others', which means that theirs is superior to yours—which means that you were wrong to say that all are equal.

DESCARTES: That is a clever sophism, Socrates.

SOCRATES: Show me how that is all it is. Answer the charge of self-contradiction.

DESCARTES: There is no contradiction. You have not shown a logical contradiction between any two sentences in my book.

SOCRATES: The contradiction is not between two things you say but between what you say and your act of saying it. If, as you say, you are not superior to others, why do you act as if you are by ignoring them, especially the ancients whose wisdom has been sifted and tested by time? Why do you invent a wholly new beginning for philosophy, a radically new kind of philosophy?

DESCARTES: Even if your charge of contradiction is true, the book itself does not contradict itself, if you confine yourself to judging the book rather than the author.

SOCRATES: But we have not yet found any good reasons to believe your first sentence, your Archimedean point. Your long lever still lacks a ground for its fulcrum.

4

Is Philosophy a Science?

DESCARTES: Socrates, I must be candid: I am deeply disappointed with you. You are full of clever refutations but you sound more like a sophist than a scientist.

SOCRATES: I am neither a sophist nor a scientist; I am a philosopher.

DESCARTES: But philosophy is a science, and therefore if you are a philosopher you are a scientist.

SOCRATES: Well, now, that depends on what we mean by "science". Tell me what you mean, please. Let us begin with some examples. Do you say that logic is a science?

DESCARTES: Yes.

SOCRATES: Do you say that love is a science?

DESCARTES: No.

SOCRATES: Is the love of wisdom a love?

DESCARTES: Yes, by definition.

SOCRATES: And is philosophy the love of wisdom?

DESCARTES: Yes, literally.

SOCRATES: Then the science of logic has proved that philosophy is not a science.

DESCARTES: I admit that love is not a science. Love is a *je ne sais qua*, an "I know not what." But surely wisdom is a science. It is ordered knowledge of first principles. Do you deny that?

SOCRATES: No. I never denied that *wisdom* was a science. I denied that *philosophy* was a science. For philosophy is not wisdom but the love of wisdom. And the love of wisdom comes under the genus "love", not the genus "wisdom". And love is not a science—as you yourself admitted.

DESCARTES: Ah, but the love of wisdom comes also under the genus "wisdom", as well as under the genus "love", and therefore it can be a science, since wisdom is a science. Is it not wisdom to love wisdom?

SOCRATES: It is indeed. Wisdom directs us to love her. But the servant directed is not the same as the mistress directing. The love of wisdom no more comes under the genus "wisdom" than the knowledge of horses comes under the genus "horses", or the act of climbing a mountain comes under the genus "mountain". Knowing horses is a knowing, not a horse; and the love of horses is a love, not a horse. So the love of wisdom is a love, not a wisdom.

DESCARTES: Socrates, I suspect you have been doing something very un-Socratic with me . . .

SOCRATES: You mean giving short, direct answers rather than long, indirect questions?

DESCARTES: Yes. Why have you changed your method?

SOCRATES: I have been tempering the wind to the shorn lamb.

DESCARTES: I feel I have been gently insulted.

SOCRATES: Would you prefer me to revert to my purer style?

DESCARTES: No. Except in one respect. You have also been un-Socratic in that you have been using terms like "wisdom", "science", and "reason" without insisting on defining them.

SOCRATES: By the Dog, so I have! *Mea culpa, mea culpa, mea maxima culpa!* What evil demon has deceived me? How utterly inexcusable of me! Well, it seems that my secret is out, then: when I said that this was your Purgatory but my Heaven, I was jesting. For if this were my Heaven, I would never have acted with such folly. No, this is purgation and purification for both of us, and we shall both err and be exposed as fools.

DESCARTES: Then if you cannot agree that wisdom is equal in all men, perhaps you will at least agree that folly is!

SOCRATES: Alas, even that can not be equal, for folly is the opposite of wisdom, so that the more folly one has, the less wisdom, and the more wisdom, the less folly. So if the one is unequal, the other must be also.

DESCARTES: Do you not agree that there is some mixture of wisdom and folly in all men?

SOCRATES: Yes, but not in the same proportions.

DESCARTES: I think we do not really disagree here, Socrates, for what I meant by the "good sense" that is equal in all men is not the same as what you mean by the "wisdom" that is unequal. That is why I reminded you that it is high time to define terms.

SOCRATES: Long *past* high time, I fear. Oh, well, they say a fool is one who learns by experience, so let this fool at least learn. Define our terms we will indeed!

DESCARTES: Did you think I meant by "good sense" the same thing you meant by "wisdom"?

SOCRATES: Yes, because I thought you had already defined it as **"the power of judging rightly and of distinguishing the true from the false"**—a definition I thought I understood and agreed with. I suppose that is why I did not insist on my usual long preliminary discussion about how to define our key term. But now I think my assumption was mistaken. So let us backtrack—often this is the only road to progress—and ask what we each mean by "the power of judging rightly and of distinguishing the true from the false".

Do you mean judging rightly and distinguishing the true from the false *about anything at all*? For instance, how to cure leprosy, and what color Homer's eyes were, and how many planets there are, and why good men suffer, and how many sixes there are in a thousand, and whether war is ever good, and whether there are many gods, or one, or none? Do you say

DM 1, para. 1

that all men are equal in their ability to judge all these things?

DESCARTES: Of course not. For only those who saw Homer can judge what color his eyes were. As to the other questions, though, I believe all men have the same innate *ability* to discover the truth about these things if only they are given the proper tools and time. What do you say about that?

SOCRATES: I say that all men are indeed equal regarding their ability to find the truth about some of these other things, but not about all of them. You distinguished the question of the color of Homer's eyes from all the other questions—rightly, I think —because only sense experience can show us what is true there, and only the few men who met Homer had that experience, so the many are not equal to the few there. But the role of sense experience in empowering us to answer the other questions is not the same, is it? Sometimes that role is nonexistent, as in the question about the numbers. At other times, it is a necessary ingredient, but needs to be supplemented by mathematical calculation, as in the question about the number of planets. Sometimes, it is necessary but needs to be supplemented by experiments, as in the question about curing leprosy. And sometimes it is necessary but needs to be supplemented by an experience that is more than sensory, and by moral wisdom, as in the questions about why good men suffer, and whether war is good. And sometimes it needs to be supplemented by facility with abstract concepts of metaphysics and complex logical reasoning, as with the question about many gods, one, or none. At least, that is how it seems to me. Do you agree?

DESCARTES: I think I see what you are up to here. You are asking about *method*, and my claim to give mankind "*the*" method for all truth, rather than the many different methods for knowing many different kinds of truths that Aristotle said were needed. Well, a method can be tested only by practice. If my claim about "the" method is true, then it will work; if it is not true, it will not work. So we can test the first claim in my book—the claim in its very title, the claim about "the" method—only by testing my uses of my new method in the rest of the book. So let us make that test now, if you please.

SOCRATES: If this is your only assumption—that your new method will work for all things—and if an assumption about method can be tested only by testing its many applications—then we must proceed to that now. But if there is a second assumption, and if that assumption is one of theory rather than practice, of truth rather than utility, then we must question that second assumption, I think. Do you not agree? Is not the very first principle of your method to question all assumptions?

DESCARTES: Yes. What is this second assumption that you say I make?

SOCRATES: Why, the very thing we have been investigating for quite a while now! Whether reason is the same in all men or not. And that is why I enumerated all these different examples of learning the truth—

about mathematics, and about war, and about leprosy —because they seem to refute that second assumption of yours.

DESCARTES: I see your logical strategy. But I do not see why you think these examples refute my assumption that reason is equal in all men. For all the mental equipment needed to find the truth in all these different places is present in every man: sense experience, mathematical ability, moral wisdom, experience of human relationships, the power to think abstractly —these are all common to all men. The only innate differences are differences in speed. That is what we mean, or ought to mean, by greater or lesser degrees of intelligence. Some men will take longer to develop these innate capacities, and some will proceed more quickly; and some will bend more will and effort to the task, while others will be lazy; and therefore some will reach the goal of truth more quickly than others. Some may even need surgery to repair physical damage to the brain. But all can reach the truth, for all possess the natural powers that are needed, and all possess these powers because these powers are all part of human nature, or the human essence; and human nature is present in all humans, not only some. That is a law of logic: the essence is present in all members of a species, while the accidents are present only in some. To put it in political terms, essence is egalitarian, not elitist; it is only accidents that are elitist. And reason is the human essence, or part of it. Therefore reason is egalitarian, not elitist. And that is my *proof* of what you call my second assumption:

DM 1,
para. 2

For as to reason or good sense, given that it alone makes us men and distinguishes us from animals, I prefer to believe that it exists whole and entire in each one of us. In this belief I am following the standard opinion held by philosophers who say that there are differences of degree only among accidents, but not among forms or natures of individuals of the same species.

So just as all triangles are equally triangular, and equally three-sided, all men are equally human, and equally rational.

SOCRATES: The logic of your argument seems faultless.

DESCARTES: Then can we proceed to the rest of the book?

SOCRATES: If you will allow me just one little additional test of this assumption of yours.

DESCARTES: What further test do you require, if the argument is faultless?

SOCRATES: The test of experience. Does experience conform to what your argument proves? Do we find in real life what the argument predicts we will find?

DESCARTES: You can see that it does. For you can see that the principles of reasoning are known to all men. There is no "Greek logic" or "French logic", no "masculine logic" or "feminine logic". There is simply logic. If all A is B and all B is C, then all A must be C, whether in Greece or in France, whether you are a man or a woman, and whether A, B, and C are animals, concepts, gods, or chemicals.

SOCRATES: Yes, but logical reasoning is only part of what we ancients meant by "reason".

DESCARTES: Obviously, we need to define our terms.

SOCRATES: That is precisely what we are doing. You have studied the philosophy of Aristotle, have you not?

DESCARTES: Yes. And I have surpassed him and corrected some of his mistakes . . .

SOCRATES: What about his logic? Have you studied his logic?

DESCARTES: Of course.

SOCRATES: Do you claim to have corrected his mistakes in logic? Have you invented a new logic?

DESCARTES: No. There is no other logic, just as there is no other geometry than Euclid's.

SOCRATES: Fine. Actually, there *is* another geometry, one that denies one of Euclid's axioms, the one about parallel lines. It was invented by a Russian named Lobaschevsky some three centuries after your death, and it works quite well. But there is no logic that can deny the axioms of noncontradiction and identity. . . .

DESCARTES: Tell me more about this Lobaschevsky, please!

SOCRATES: Tomorrow, perhaps. One thing at a time, please, one day at a time, and one book at a time.

Now, do you recall that in his logic Aristotle distinguished *three* "acts of the mind" that constitute reason and raise man's mind above the animals?

DESCARTES: Of course. This is elementary.

SOCRATES: Do you recall what the "three acts of the mind" are?

DESCARTES: Of course: understanding the meaning of a concept, judging the truth of a proposition that links two concepts as subject and predicate, and reasoning to the truth of a conclusion from the assumption of certain premises. And the first and third acts of the mind are means to the end of truth, which is found only in the second act of the mind, judging. Defining terms and reasoning are both means of finding truth, while it is *propositions* that are true or false. Terms are only clear or unclear, and arguments are only logically valid or fallacious.

SOCRATES: Exactly. And when *you* speak of "reason", you speak only of the third act of the mind, or perhaps the second and third together, but not the first, not understanding. Perhaps understanding is not equal in all men, even though the other powers are.

DESCARTES: Actually, the terminology of the "three acts of the mind" comes from the medieval Scholastic philosophers, not Aristotle.

SOCRATES: But the distinguishing of these three acts is in Aristotle, is it not?—though in different words.

DESCARTES: Yes, but the different words are important because terminology itself sometimes prevents progress. For instance, take Aristotle's terminology of the "four causes". The distinctions he makes are valid, but they held back the progress of the physical sciences for centuries by insisting that the "final cause", or purpose, of anything was "the cause of causes" and the supreme explanation. Science went hunting for final causes and found only the uncertain, the questionable, the subjective. Only when science set aside those categories and changed its terminology did it begin to make progress. I do not take Aristotle for my authority, either in science or in philosophy. For philosophy may mislead science. And in philosophy I have always preferred Plato to Aristotle. As I thought you would too.

SOCRATES: Then let us use Plato's categories. Do you recall the "divided line" at the end of Book 6 of the *Republic*?

DESCARTES: Of course. Why do you bring that up?

SOCRATES: Because it was Plato's map of the levels of knowing, and the levels of education, which he then portrayed dramatically in the parable of the escape from the cave of ignorance into the light of certainty, at the beginning of Book 7.

DESCARTES: The most memorable image in the history of philosophy! And one that I identify with personally because I fulfill this escape from the cave precisely by my method. Plato would welcome me as his best ally.

SOCRATES: And do you remember how Plato then details these four steps of education in the rest of Book 7 by laying out the curriculum for his Academy—a curriculum that has persisted for two thousand years, and that was the map for your own education?

DESCARTES: Of course.

SOCRATES: How do you understand those four steps, in clear and ordinary language?

DESCARTES: We begin by doubting nothing, by accepting all appearances as true, all images and pictures and opinions about things, without questioning the images by demanding to know the things of which they are the images. You see, the first step of my method—doubt—is precisely the first step of Plato's education: the demand to climb farther up the ladder, to question the shadows on the wall of the cave, to question all authority and tradition and settled opinions—which is exactly what you yourself did in every one of your dialogues, Socrates!

SOCRATES: Indeed—and that is why I am doing it still, to you.

DESCARTES: Oh. You mean you are questioning the value of questioning? You are doubting the value of doubting everything, which is the first rule of my method?

SOCRATES: No, that would be moving too fast. We are not yet investigating the four rules of your method, for we have not yet read that far into your book. We are investigating only what you mean by "reason". And this first and lowest level of Plato's "divided line" is the first and lowest level of reason. To trust images, whether physical or mental, to trust pictures and to trust conventional opinions, that is, to trust the authority of tradition—is this not how we all begin to learn when we are children? We later question them, but if we did not begin with them we could not question them. I too always began my dialogues by asking the other for his opinions, and only then did I question them. How could one proceed to the second level of the line unless one began on the first level?

DESCARTES: Do you mean to say that even the uncritical belief in images, the shadows on the wall of the cave, are part of "reason"?

SOCRATES: I do.

DESCARTES: But that does not distinguish men from animals. Animals too believe in and live by appearances. I don't understand how you could call that "reason".

SOCRATES: That is very simple: when we ancients defined man as "the rational animal", we included in that term "reason" all those powers that we found in our experience that distinguished men from animals. And that included such uncritical things as moral conscience, the uncritical awareness of good and evil; and aesthetic sensibility, the uncritical awareness of beauty and ugliness; and the ability to read human hearts and faces intuitively; and even the intuitive awareness of something religious, something to worship, some sort of gods. Animals cannot do any of these things. Yet these things are all immediate "appearances", but not *sensory* appearances. They are immediate appearances to our *reason*.

DESCARTES: I see what you mean. And the second level of the line, the sense experience of the actual physical things in the world—how does that distinguish men from animals?

SOCRATES: By distinguishing itself from the first level, that is, by distinguishing reality from appearances. We question these appearances and test them. On the sensory level, we test pictures and images by the direct sense experience of the things that caused these images. After we see the shadows, we wonder what real things caused them. That is how we begin to educate ourselves. The cave dwellers turn their heads around to see the objects that cast the shadows. They do that only because they wonder about it. They become philosophers. (Philosophy begins in wonder.) They become truth seekers, just for the sake of seeing truth. Animals do not do that. Animals do not become philosophers. Their curiosity is only practical.

DESCARTES: I see. We then have a dramatic interpretation of Plato's "divided line" rather than a static one: it is not so much the levels themselves but the movement upwards from one to the other that makes for "reason".

SOCRATES: Yes. And therefore "reason" encompasses all four levels. The learner moves from the first level, the images of things, to the second level, to things themselves, and then from the second level to the third, from the things to the laws and principles that explain things. These are the principles of mathematics and logic, especially the principles of reasoning from premises to conclusions, from hypotheses to consequences, from "if" to "then". And this, I think, is what *you* mean by the "reason" that is equal in all men. It is the third level of Plato's line.

DESCARTES: Yes. That is why I said there is no Greek logic or French logic, just logic.

SOCRATES: And you are clearly right there. And the modern scientific method, which you helped formulate, is basically the combination of these two levels of Plato's line, the sense experience of level two; and the mathematical measurement and reasoning of level three.

DESCARTES: I would rather say that it is two *movements*, two demands: first, the demand for movement from level one to level two, which is the demand to verify the appearances or impressions or opinions on level one by sense experience on level two; and, second, the demand for movement from level two to level three, the demand to judge the sense experiences of the physical things on level two by the mathematical and logical principles and laws that constitute level three. Francis Bacon emphasized the first of these two movements, and that was the empirical part of the scientific method. I emphasized the second movement, the mathematical part.

I believe old Pythagoras was right: mathematics is the language of nature, and therefore mathematical measurement, mathematical principles, and mathematical reasoning is the key to certainty in all the physical sciences.

SOCRATES: I think that is what Plato meant by the symbol of the fire inside the cave. The fire is the

light of the cave, the light that clarifies the physical
world. But it is only the light of the physical world,
not of the higher world outside the cave. So I do not
see how your mathematical method can be a *universal*
method. We can measure physical things by quantity,
but not spiritual things. We cannot measure God or
the soul with a tape measure.

DESCARTES: But we can still use the mathematical
method of reasoning about them and thus attain certainty and overcome these differences of opinion that
have plagued philosophy from the earliest times.

SOCRATES: Do you think we can do that when we
reach the fourth level of the "line"? Can we use mathematical and logical reasoning to know and judge the
essences of things?

DESCARTES: Certainly. You did that very thing yourself—or Plato did. You did some very exact reasoning
about justice in the *Republic*.

SOCRATES: In Book I, yes. But remember the ending
of Book I: I was dissatisfied with it precisely because
it did not reach the fourth level, the understanding
of the essential Form of justice.

DESCARTES: Perhaps that is why Plato did not discover the scientific method: he tried to do too much,
he tried to include too much in "reason". As you said,
Socrates, "reason" meant all four levels of the "line"
to you and to him and to most of you ancient philosophers. By excluding the lowest and highest levels
of Plato's line, and by combining the other two, we
moderns created the scientific method.

It is like concentrating together soldiers who had previously been scattered on a battlefield, to form a tight and narrow phalanx, so that they could succeed, in their "narrowness", where they had failed in their "broadness". Or it is like a spotlight concentrating its light on one player on the stage, and thus concentrating the audience's attention on that one player, for instance while Hamlet is speaking his soliloquy "To be or not to be, that is the question", rather than having a floodlight illumine all parts of the stage at the same time with a weaker intensity. This method of "narrowing" reason has worked with remarkable success in all the sciences.

SOCRATES: Yes, it has. But can it work in philosophy? To be or not to be scientific in philosophy, *that* is the question.

DESCARTES: I answer: to be. That is why I wrote my book. I believed that your beloved master Plato was wrong when he thought that each level of his "line" required a different kind of thought and a different method.

SOCRATES: Plato came to his conclusion after much experience. Your opposite conclusion seems to be an assumption a priori.

DESCARTES: It is neither. It is a hypothesis, to be tested. And my book is its test.

SOCRATES: Then we must test your test.

DESCARTES: It's about time! Why do you talk about doing a thing for such a long time before you do it?

SOCRATES: Perhaps it is because I am like Hamlet. Or perhaps it is because I am just overpatient—impatient with impatience, one might say. Or perhaps it is because we have no lack of time here. Or, most likely of all, perhaps it is because I want us to be much more careful and clear about our thinking than we usually are.

DESCARTES: In other words, because you agree with the fundamental demand of my method. I think we are much akin, Socrates. What do you think?

SOCRATES: I think we should not be so hasty. Perhaps. We shall see in the end.

5

Descartes' Hidden Agenda

SOCRATES: Part One of your book is a charming and enlightening little intellectual autobiography, in which your readers are invited to share the story of your two discoveries: of the need for a new method and of the method that supplied that need. I have just one or two little questions about it.

DESCARTES: I am not surprised to hear you say that.

SOCRATES: You say:

> **But I shall have no fear of declaring that I think I have been fortunate.** [Your discovery *must* have been due to fortune rather than your own intellectual powers, since all men are equal in their intellectual power of reason, according to your own first principle.] **I have, since my youth, found myself on paths that have led me to certain considerations and maxims from which I have formed a method by means of which, it seems to me, I have the ways to increase my knowledge by degrees and to raise it gradually to the highest point to which the mediocrity of my mind and the short span of my life can allow it to attain.**

DM 1, para. 3

[Later in the book you will address both of these obstacles to knowledge, the mediocrity of the mind and the short span of life, in one stroke, when you write, **"The mind depends so greatly upon the temperament and on the disposition of the organs of the body that, were it possible to find some means to make men generally more wise and competent than they have been up until now, I believe that one should look to medicine to find this means."** But more about that later.]

For I have already reaped from it such a harvest that, though as regards judgments I make of myself, I try always to lean toward caution rather than toward presumption, . . . I always take immense satisfaction in the progress that I think I have made in the search for truth.

DM 1,
para. 3

I think I might have just a few questions about your "immense satisfaction"—something I longed for all my life yet never came even close to attaining. So if you can teach me the way to this "immense satisfaction" that I have so longed for, I shall be eternally in your debt.

DESCARTES: I recognize your irony, Socrates. You think I am unwise, perhaps even arrogant, for claiming so much for my method, in contrast to your "wisdom", which was your recognition that you had no wisdom. But I say in the very next paragraph, **"All the same, it could be that I am mistaken."**

DM 1,
para. 4

SOCRATES: I am happy to hear that you do not believe it is impossible that you may be mistaken. Surely you may rightly take "immense satisfaction" in such humility!

DESCARTES: I am sorry you do not believe in my humility.

SOCRATES: Oh, I believe in your *belief* in your humility.

DESCARTES: But my next paragraph shows how humble my claim really is:

Thus my purpose here is not to teach the method that everyone ought to follow in order to conduct his reason correctly, but merely to show how I have tried to conduct mine.

DM 1,
para. 5

SOCRATES: Did you really mean that?

DESCARTES: I think so. (I find that I cannot lie in this place!) That is why I entitled my longer book *Meditations*. It is a series of meditations or thought experiments that can be done only by each individual, one at a time, in the privacy of his own thoughts.

SOCRATES: How then can it be scientific if it is so personal?

DESCARTES: Because science too is an enterprise that must be done by individuals, though of course they share the results of their experiments with others and invite other individuals to replicate them. That is exactly what I did, in the laboratory of my own mind.

SOCRATES: But science seeks truths that are objective and universal and impersonal.

DESCARTES: Indeed. And so does philosophy. But the act of seeking is subjective and individual and personal.

SOCRATES: True. So when you wrote, **"Thus my purpose here is not to teach the method that everyone ought to follow"**, you really meant that?

DESCARTES: Of course.

SOCRATES: But when you added, **"but merely to show how I have tried to conduct mine"**, you did not.

DESCARTES: Why do you say that?

SOCRATES: I will answer that question by asking you one: Did you write to no readers, to some, or to all?

DESCARTES: To some: to all who wish to philosophize.

SOCRATES: And these readers are invited to replicate your thought experiment?

DESCARTES: Yes.

SOCRATES: And what do you claim is new in this thought experiment of yours? What profit can these readers derive from your thoughts that they could not derive from others, especially from the philosophers of the past?

DESCARTES: Certainty—and universal agreement, the ending of differences of opinion.

SOCRATES: Do you think these are desirable goals?

DESCARTES: Of course.

SOCRATES: And do we all desire them?

DESCARTES: Yes.

SOCRATES: And why can your readers attain these universally desired goals from your philosophy better than from other philosophies?

DESCARTES: We saw the answer to that question already, Socrates. In one word, the answer is "the method". I do not have a superior mind, and I do not have a distinctively new set of philosophical conclusions—I prove the existence of the self, soul, God, body, and world that we all knew existed—but I have found a better method.

SOCRATES: And what makes it better? What is its difference from previous methods?

DESCARTES: It is truly scientific.

SOCRATES: And what is the difference between true science and true autobiography?

DESCARTES: Autobiography reveals particular truths about a particular individual, while science discovers universal truths that are objective and impersonal, even though the *search* for them is personal.

SOCRATES: So when you say that you write only to show how you have conducted your own thoughts and not to tell others how to conduct theirs, you are claiming only autobiographical truth, not scientific truth.

DESCARTES: Of course. But some will choose to walk the same path as I have walked, to perform the same thought experiments, and, hopefully, attain the same results. But the decision to be scientific and to seek objective truth must be a subjective, personal choice. I see no contradiction here, or even any problem. Do you?

SOCRATES: I think I do. I am trying to "read between the lines", as they say, to understand more clearly your intention in this book. And I think I do see a contradiction if we read only the lines themselves that you have written rather than your unwritten intentions.

DESCARTES: Where?

SOCRATES: In Part Two, where you again say, in more detail, what you said in Part One, in your very first sentence, the sentence we have been examining for a long time now. In fact, your wording in Part Two seems explicitly designed to contradict your first sentence of Part One. It is in the third paragraph of Part Two, where you write:

DM 2, para. 3

> This is why I could not approve of all of those trouble-making and quarrelsome types who, called neither by birth nor by fortune to manage public affairs, never cease in their imagination to effect some new reformation. [*That* word was a flash point for religious warfare in your day.] And if I thought there were the slightest thing in this essay by means of which one might suspect me of such folly, I would be very sorry to permit its publication.
>
> My plan has never been more than to try to reform my own thoughts and to build upon a foundation which is completely my own.

And if, my work having sufficiently pleased
me, I show it to you here as a model, it is not
for that reason that I wish to advise anyone
to imitate it. . . . The world consists almost
completely of but two kinds of people and
for these two kinds it is not at all suitable:
namely (1) those who, believing themselves
more capable than they really are, cannot
help making premature judgments . . . (and)
(2) as for those people who have enough reason or modesty to judge that they are less capable to distinguish the true from the false
than are others by whom they can be instructed, they ought to content themselves
more with following the opinions of these
others than to look for better opinions on
their own.

Now here is something very puzzling. These two
classes of people who you here say should *not* use your
method—they are exactly the two classes of people
who do not *exist*, according to what you say in your
very first paragraph in Part One!

First, **"those who believe themselves more capable than they really are"**. No one fits that description, according to your first paragraph, where
you say that **"each of us considers himself to be
so well endowed . . . with it** [good sense] **that even
those who are the most difficult to please in all
other matters are not wont to desire more of it
than they have."** And then you say that "**it is not
likely that anyone is mistaken about this fact."**
Put these two statements together and you get the

conclusion that everyone has equal "good sense" or "capability to judge and to distinguish the true from the false", and knows it, and is satisfied with it. So *no* one believes himself to be more capable than he really is regarding this power of reason or good sense.

And the second class of people with no one in it is the second class of people who you say should not use your book, **"those people who have enough reason** (But don't we all have enough? Don't we all have an equal amount? You said we did.) **to judge that they are less capable to distinguish the true from the false than are others."** But in paragraph one of Part One you said that **"the power of judging rightly and of distinguishing the true from the false (which, properly speaking, is what people call good sense or reason) is naturally equal in all men."** But if all are equal, then no one is less capable of reason than anyone else.

Your very choice of words is repeated exactly, so that the attentive reader will remember the earlier paragraph when he reads the later one. **"La puissance de bien juger et distinguer le vrai d'avec le faux, qui est proprement ce qu'on nomme le bon sens ou la raison"** is what you say is equal in all, in Part One. But then in Part Two you say, **"Puis de ceux qui, ayant assez de raison . . . pour juger qu'ils sone moins capables de distinguer le vrai d'avec le faux que quelques autres."** So some have less reason than others.

Since you are a very intelligent and logical man, this clear contradiction could not be an oversight. It must be a deliberate clue. But to what?

DESCARTES: Socrates, surely you are intelligent enough to answer that question. Which of these two passages do you think I really believe, and which do you think I put in as a sop for the censors, who fear anything new if it goes beyond the private and is propagated among the public as some new "reform", especially in an age when the Reformation had produced the bloodiest war in history? You above all men should understand that. I put that paragraph into Part Two to avoid your fate, Socrates.

SOCRATES: Of course! You would not have written the book at all if you did not think it could reform thoughts. And not just private thoughts, for your new method is just the opposite of a private method for only a few individuals; it is the scientific method, which is public and for all. This was your solution to the dilemma: either publish these radically new thoughts and be persecuted by the fools who try to kill ideas by killing people—or else withhold them from the human race, withhold the way these very fools can be tamed by reason and perhaps even the way by which all wars of ideas can cease.

DESCARTES: Congratulations, Socrates. Your perspicacity has discovered my strategy. I planted just enough clues in my book so that foxes like you would find them, but dogs like the censors would not.

And here is another clue for the wise: at the beginning of Part Two, from which you quoted my paragraph about "reformation", I tell of my experience of witnessing this devastating war of religion, which had been caused by passionate differences in opinion. And what did I offer my new method as therapy for, as salvation from? Differences of opinion! And I say these are curable, for they are caused not by innate differences in reason among different people, but only by the use of different "approaches" or methods. Take away the cause and you will take away the effect. Take away the differences in methods and you will take away the differences in opinion. Take away the differences in opinion and you will take away the religious wars.

So you see why my book was important, and why I could not publish it until the Galileo incident was forgotten, or at least quiet. And why, when I did publish it, I had to insert sops for the censors and hidden clues for the wise. I want to be a good and honest man, and a public benefactor, but I had no desire or calling to be a martyr like you.

6

Knowledge's Goal

SOCRATES: I quite understand now why you concealed your rather radical and revolutionary goals from the existing political powers, while at the same time suggesting these goals in a hidden way that intelligent readers could notice. (I know how unintelligent political censors can be!) Yet you do reveal quite a bit of your radical new demands in your autobiographical account of your academic life, especially your deep dissatisfaction with all of the philosophy of the past, especially the medieval Scholastic philosophy taught to you by the Jesuits, the best teachers of your age.

DESCARTES: Ah, yes. The clergy picked quarrels with me on everything I wrote and tried to get my books condemned by the Church. Yet I was only trying to found the basic beliefs we both shared on a new and stronger foundation, especially the two crucial religious beliefs of the existence of the God and the immateriality and immortality of the soul.

SOCRATES: A similar thing happened to me. My philosophy too was new in method, but not in content. I too sought a stronger, more rational ground for traditional beliefs—and was misunderstood and feared

for it. So I follow you in spirit on your journey—so
far, at least. Let us explore more of your road, then.

You write: **"I had been raised on letters** [*lettres*,
books] **from my childhood, and because I was con-**
DM 1,   **vinced that through them one might acquire a**
para. 6 **clear and steady** [*assure*, assured, guaranteed, cer-
tain] **knowledge of everything that is useful** [*utile*]
for life, I possessed a tremendous desire to learn
them."

Already in this first sentence we meet three reasons
for your dissatisfaction with the Scholastic philosophy you learned from your teachers—in fact, with
all previous philosophy. You sought a philosophy
based on personal experience rather than books, one
that was certain rather than probable, and one that
was not just theoretical but practical, or useful.

DESCARTES: You understand me very well, Socrates.
Do you also understand how these three are related?

SOCRATES: I think so. You believed that only certain
knowledge was really useful, and that only a knowledge based on one's own experience rather than on
trust in the authors of books could be certain.

DESCARTES: We are indeed kindred spirits.

SOCRATES: Somewhat, at least. The first of your three
demands seems very similar to mine. In terms of
Plato's "divided line" that we have already spoken
of, the first step, which he called knowing images, is
like your "letters" (books), I think. Although Plato
meant by the objects on this lowest level only *physi-*
cal images like pictures or reflections in a mirror, it
could also be used for the *mental* images or opinions

in other minds. This kind of knowing is handed down from others. It relies on intermediaries, on tradition and trust in the authority of those who formed it. Like me, you wanted to see for yourself by your own experience (whether that experience was sensory or intellectual). You were not satisfied to trust the intermediaries unquestioningly, which in your case were not simply pictures but books and teachers and tradition. That dissatisfaction is the first step in critical rational inquiry.

DESCARTES: And like Plato, I did not expect everyone to take that first step. Faith in the intermediaries who hand down the tradition has always sufficed for most men. I did not expect to make all men philosophers.

SOCRATES: Actually, I did. I was more egalitarian than Plato. I invited everyone I met to philosophize, even Meno's totally uneducated slave boy. I brought him up to the next level of the "divided line" by a certain mathematical deduction, if you remember.

DESCARTES: What reader of the "Meno" could forget that wonderful example of teaching? So I think we also agree about the need for the next step, from level two to level three, from sensory experience to the certainty of mathematics.

SOCRATES: Yes, but I think we differ about the fourth and highest level, philosophical wisdom, which is a kind of intellectual intuition into what Plato called the Forms, the essences. That was my ultimate goal, and the highest kind of certainty, one that did not depend on premises, as mathematics does.

DESCARTES: But philosophers continually disagree about wisdom, about the essences. So this is *not* a more certain knowledge than mathematics.

SOCRATES: So I think we differ about where to find your goal of certainty. And I think we also differ about goal of practicality. You sought **"an assured knowledge of everything that is useful for life"**, while I sought the truth for its own sake. You sought a logically certain scientific knowledge of the changing things in this world so that you could use them and control them and improve them. You were a Baconian rather than an Aristotelian, not only about the method of knowing but also about the goal of knowing. You believed in Bacon's "knowledge for power". You sought "man's conquest of nature".

DESCARTES: I can hardly expect you to share my enthusiasm for the conquest of nature, Socrates. You ancients had no idea of the potentialities of technology.

SOCRATES: Potentialities for what?

DESCARTES: For human progress.

SOCRATES: Perhaps not, but I did have a pretty clear idea of the need for defining terms. That term "progress", for instance. What do you mean by that?

DESCARTES: I explain it in some detail in Part Six of my book. I meant progress in understanding nature (especially that part of nature closest to us, our own bodies) so that we can conquer it, control it, improve it, and use it **"for the relief of man's estate"**.

SOCRATES: The relief from what?

DESCARTES: Suffering. Do you deny that that is a worthy end?

SOCRATES: No. But . . .

DESCARTES: I knew you would have a big "but".

SOCRATES: That is because you are very logical. If I have a big waist, it follows that I must have a big butt. But by *suffering* do you mean *pain*?

DESCARTES: Yes.

SOCRATES: And pain is the opposite of pleasure?

DESCARTES: Yes.

SOCRATES: Do you believe that pleasure is the greatest good?

DESCARTES: No.

SOCRATES: Then how can the relief from pain be the greatest good?

DESCARTES: I do not say it is the greatest good. It is only one part of a greater good, namely, human happiness.

SOCRATES: I think you can guess what my next question is going to be.

DESCARTES: What is happiness?

SOCRATES: Yes. Is it not the fulfillment of all human desires? Would you accept that definition of happiness?

DESCARTES: It is the common meaning of the term.

SOCRATES: So the conquest of nature (which men will call "technology") increases happiness by bending

nature to the will of man and satisfying human desires—is that the reason the conquest of nature makes
for happiness?

DESCARTES: That seems to be the connection.

SOCRATES: And happiness is the greatest good?

DESCARTES: Yes. Everyone seeks everything else as a
means to the goal of happiness, while no one seeks
happiness as a means to any other goal.

SOCRATES: We ancients thought that happiness, or
the greatest good, consisted in conforming the human soul to objective reality—for instance, by the
knowledge of the truth for its own sake, and by conforming our desires to the truth by the virtues of
practical wisdom and justice and courage and self-
control. But you are saying that the greatest good
consists in conforming objective reality to the desires
of the soul. In other words, that power is a greater
good than knowledge.

DESCARTES: No, no, I do not say that power is the
greatest good. Happiness is the greatest good.

SOCRATES: But you rank power as closer to the greatest good than knowledge, for you say that knowledge
is a means to power and that power over nature is a
means to happiness.

DESCARTES: Yes.

SOCRATES: Then we are far less spiritually akin than
you think.

7

The Search for Certainty

SOCRATES: To continue with your story, you write:

I had been raised on letters from my childhood, and because I was convinced that through them one might acquire a clear and steady knowledge of everything that is useful for life, I possessed a tremendous desire to learn them. But as soon as I completed this entire course of study, at the end of which one is ordinarily received into the ranks of the learned, I changed my mind entirely. For I was embarrassed by so many doubts and errors. . . .

DM 1,
para. 6

I think I should pause here to investigate these two words, "doubts" and "errors", since these summarized your critique of the two thousand years of philosophy before you, and what you hoped to attain in your new philosophy.

DESCARTES: Fair enough. These were the two spurs that moved my quest, as spurs move a horse. I was a knight of the mind—as you were, Socrates.

SOCRATES: If you were dissatisfied with doubts, you must have been seeking the opposite of doubts, is it not so?

77

DESCARTES: Yes.

SOCRATES: And what is the opposite of doubt?

DESCARTES: Certainty, or indubitability. This was the attribute I found lacking in traditional philosophy. Many of these ideas may have been true, as well as profound and useful, but I could not *know* that they were true, but only *opine*.

SOCRATES: And did you ever find the attribute you sought, indubitability, anywhere in your education?

DESCARTES: I did.

SOCRATES: Where?

DESCARTES: In only one subject: mathematics.

SOCRATES: And did you ever find any philosopher before you who believed that *philosophy* could attain the certainty, or the kind of certainty, or the degree of certainty, that you found in mathematics?

DESCARTES: No one.

SOCRATES: But *you* thought that *you* could find that kind of certainty in philosophy?

DESCARTES: Yes.

SOCRATES: Why?

DESCARTES: Because all the others did philosophy not as one does science but as one does religion: by accepting the authority of tradition. Almost all Christian philosophers accepted the authority of either "the divine Plato" or of "*the* Philosopher", the great Aristotle, who had taught that each science had to have its own method and its own different degree of certainty. This was the assumption I questioned. So I was questioning the near infallibility of Aristotle.

SOCRATES: Speaking of "infallibility", the second thing you said you were "embarrassed" by was *errors*, was it not?

DESCARTES: Yes.

SOCRATES: And errors come from fallibility, do they not?

DESCARTES: Yes.

SOCRATES: And the opposite of fallibility, is infallibility, is it not?

DESCARTES: Yes.

SOCRATES: So you were seeking for infallibility, freedom from all error. And in philosophy, no less. You say you wanted philosophy to imitate science instead of religion, but now it seems that you wanted to give philosophy something like the infallibility of divine revelation! I can see why you feared the censors.

DESCARTES: But the ground of infallibility in religion is wholly different from the ground of infallibility in mathematical science. In religion it is the authority of God. In mathematics it is the self-evidence of tautologies like $X = X$ or $2 + 2 = 4$.

SOCRATES: I see. Well, let's continue your story.

I was embarrassed by so many doubts and errors, which appeared in no way to profit me in my attempt at learning, except that more and more I discovered my ignorance. And nevertheless, I was in one of the most cel- DM 1, para. 6

ebrated schools in Europe, where I thought
there ought to be learned men—if in fact
there were any such men in the world. I
learned everything the others learned; and,
not judging the disciplines taught there to
be enough, I even went through every book
I could lay my hands on that treated those
disciplines considered the most curious and
unusual . . . yet I never ceased admiring the
academic exercises with which we occupied
ourselves in school . . .

What seems "curious and unusual" to *me* is what
you next say about each of the disciplines you learned.
You seem to praise each one for something quite
different from what that discipline *ought* to provide.
"Damning with faint praise" is what this is called, I
think.

DESCARTES: Excuse me for interrupting, Socrates, but
I need to explain two things to you before you ana-
lyze what I next say about each discipline. First, my
appreciation for all of them was genuine, not sar-
castic. And, second, each of them lacked what I was
looking for, namely, the certainty that I found only
in one discipline, mathematics. My claim is that I
have found the way to extend to all the other disciplines the certainty that I found there: through my
new method, which is the main point of this book,
and of my philosophy, and of my life's contribution
to mankind, I think.

SOCRATES: Thank you for that clarification. Now let
us run through your list of all the disciplines of hu-

man knowledge as you found them in your university, and the common lack of certainty in all of them:

1. **I realized that the languages one learns are necessary for the understanding of classical texts;**
2. **that the gracefulness of fables awakens the mind;**
3. [that] **memorable deeds** [recounted in histories] **sustain it, and, read with discretion, aid in forming one's judgment;**
4. **that reading good books is like a conversation with the noblest people of past centuries — their authors — indeed, even a studied conversation in which they uncover only the best of their thoughts;**
5. **that poetry has a ravishing delicacy and sweetness;**
6. **that eloquence has incomparable power and beauty;**
7. **that mathematics contains very subtle inventions that can serve as much to satisfy the curious as to facilitate the arts and to diminish man's labor;**
8. **that writings dealing with morals contain many lessons and exhortations to virtue which are quite useful;**
9. **that theology teaches one how to go to heaven . . .**

Incidentally, you must have realized that you were misrepresenting both theology and morality here. For both claim to give us *knowledge*, and even some proofs; but you praise them only for preaching useful sermons!

DESCARTES: I was not misrepresenting the morals and theology that I learned. Both were lacking in the certainty they claimed to deliver.

SOCRATES: I see. So this *was* a "left-handed compliment", or "damning with faint praise"—a criticism disguised as a compliment.

DESCARTES: Yes. And that is so especially of philosophy, the next subject that I mention. You will notice how much it resembled the philosophy of your opponents the Sophists rather than what you tried to set against them—genuine proofs:

> 10. **that philosophy provides the means of speaking with probability about all things and of being held in admiration by the less learned;**
> 11. **that law, medicine, and the other sciences bestow honors and riches on those who cultivate them.**

Of all these disciplines, I found only one that gave me certainty:

DM 1,
para. 10

> **I took especially great pleasure in mathematics because of the certainty and the evidence of its arguments. But I did not yet notice its true usefulness and, thinking that it seemed useful only to the mechanical arts, I was astonished that, although its foundations were so solid and firm, no one had built anything more noble [*relevé*] on them.**

On the other hand, I compared the writings of the ancient pagans who discuss morals to very proud and magnificent palaces that are built on nothing but sand and mud. They place virtues on a high plateau and make them appear to be valued more than anything else in the world but they do not sufficiently instruct us about how to know [*connaître*] them; and often what they call by such a fine-sounding name is nothing more than insensibility, pride, despair, or parricide.

You see, it was as if I saw two visions, side by side: the first was the vision of these beautiful palaces, such as your own moral philosophy, Socrates, sitting on sand, or even clouds, rather than on solid ground; and the second was the vision of one truly solid and immovable foundation, mathematical reasoning, like an immense slab of rock on which only a few little sheds had been built. The invitation to combine these two pictures was irresistible: to move the old palaces onto the new foundation, or—to say the same thing differently—to move the new foundation over to the old palaces.

That is what I believe you too attempted, Socrates, in your day and with the tools you had available.

SOCRATES: What "tools" do you mean?

DESCARTES: Why, *your* new method, of course—which was in your day the same kind of revolution as my new method was in mine, but on a more primitive level. We both sought to put a more exact and certain foundation under the temples of wisdom that we inherited from our cultures. You changed the foundation from myth to logic, from tradition to reason, from faith in authority to the demand for proof. And I changed logic and reason and proof itself to something more exact and certain by taking my clue from mathematics.

You see, we both realized three things as no one else in our time did: the importance of knowledge for life, especially moral life; the importance of science for knowledge; and the importance of method for science.

You did agree with all three of these theses, did you not? You clearly taught the first one, the importance of knowledge for life, especially moral life, in your dialogues, didn't you?

SOCRATES: I did.

DESCARTES: And you said to me just a few minutes ago that you believed the scientific method was the single most important discovery in the history of science, so you must agree about the importance of method for science.

SOCRATES: I do.

DESCARTES: Then do you also agree with my remaining thesis, about the importance of science for philosophy? For if you do, then it seems only a small step to also agreeing with my use of the scientific method for philosophy.

SOCRATES: I do not know whether your scientific method will work for philosophy or not—not until I investigate your attempt to do it. Perhaps it will, perhaps it will not. Perhaps your new method will save philosophy, and perhaps it will destroy it, as *my* new method of thinking logically destroyed the credibility of the old myths. In fact that is exactly what your countryman Auguste Comte taught, three centuries after you: that philosophy replaced religion rather than saving it, in my time (he equated all religion with myth); and that science replaced philosophy rather than saving it, in your time. As an atheist he welcomed this double death, but others mourned it, and still others doubted that either of the two patients had died.

DESCARTES: What do you think about this, Socrates?

SOCRATES: I think that perhaps you are right and perhaps you are wrong. Perhaps philosophy needs a method that is as distinct from that of the natural sciences as it is from myth. That is one of the things we shall try to find out by judging your thought experiment: Can philosophy be done by the scientific method, as you tried to do it, or not?

DESCARTES: The proof of the pudding is in the eating. We shall find out how edible my philosophy is when we examine it. So far, we have been examining only its preliminaries.

SOCRATES: Are you getting impatient?

DESCARTES: No. And that surprises me. In my life on earth, impatience was a fault I frequently discovered in myself. But here it seems to be impossible. Time itself seems different here.

SOCRATES: Perhaps it is only your attitude toward it that is different.

DESCARTES: You know, Augustine doubted that there was any such thing as time in itself without some mental attitude, some mind to measure it. Is time objective or subjective or both?

SOCRATES: We must resist the temptation to explore that side road now. There will be plenty of time for it later. Back to your book, and to your defense of it, and to your three assumptions—the importance of method for science, science for knowledge, and knowledge for life. I agree with the first and last points and am now questioning the middle one.

DESCARTES: Why do you disagree with it?

SOCRATES: I did not say I disagreed with it. I am *questioning* it, to see whether I ought to agree or to disagree. And I think I must agree with it in one sense, at least. For science—in the broader sense in which we ancients used the term—consists in giving good reasons, so as to transform mere opinion or belief into knowledge. Now perhaps your mathematical method is the best way to do that, and perhaps not. Perhaps my nonmathematical reasoning can do more than your more mathematical reasoning, perhaps not. But in any case, method is important for science and science is important for knowledge. And your third point, that knowledge is important for human life, must be true, for nothing is properly human if not accompanied by knowledge. Perhaps knowledge is not *sufficient* of itself for a moral life, as I thought it was, but it is certainly *necessary*. And this is true whether knowledge is only a means to a higher end or whether it is itself the highest end; whether its good is merely an *aid* to life, a utility, as you moderns tend to believe, or whether it is a great good in itself, as we ancients believed.

DESCARTES: But surely that makes a great difference!

SOCRATES: Indeed it does. In fact, it makes a total difference, for it is the question of the *summum bonum*, the greatest good, the ultimate end and purpose of human life. Were we ancients right when we believed that the greatest good was the conforming of our thoughts and actions to objective reality by means of wisdom and virtue? Or were you moderns right when you believed that the greatest good was the conforming of objective reality to our thoughts and desires by means of technology? Is knowledge for truth, as Aristotle said, or for power, as Bacon said? What question could make a greater difference than that? But both sides say that knowledge is the primary thing needed, whether for its own sake or as a means to wisdom and virtue, or as a means to science and technology.

But the question I want to raise now is not whether you moderns are right or wrong about the *summum bonum*—that is far too large a question for our present capacities—but rather whether we both—ancients and moderns—are right or wrong about the primacy of knowledge.

DESCARTES: Do you mean to suggest that perhaps knowledge is less important than we think? I am amazed to hear *you* suggest that, Socrates, you of all people. How could that be?

SOCRATES: Well, it is only a "perhaps", but it is one that we should not leave unexamined, if we obey the first rule of your method, to assume nothing and doubt everything.

DESCARTES: Examine away, then. But what could the alternative possibly be?

SOCRATES: It might be the thing believed by most of the philosophers of the Middle Ages, Christian and Jewish and Muslim. Most of them would say, first, that knowledge is not as important as *charity*; and, second, that knowledge by science is not as important or even as certain as the knowledge that comes by *faith*, if there is in fact a revelation of knowledge from God, a God who can neither deceive nor be deceived. And they would say, in the third place, that knowledge is not as important as *wisdom*, that science is not as important as philosophy; and also, in the fourth place, that *certainty* in knowledge is not as necessary as you say it is.

DESCARTES: So they would somewhat demote the knowledge that I have exalted.

SOCRATES: Only compared to what they claim is a higher good. And they would also exalt the knowledge that you have demoted.

DESCARTES: What? How can that be, if they have demoted what I have exalted?

SOCRATES: Because they say that knowledge is *more* important than you take it to be. You seek it as a means to the further end of the conquest of nature by science and technology. They would say it is an end in itself: that perfecting the self by theoretical wisdom, and perfecting one's life by practical wisdom, is more important than perfecting the material world by technology.

DESCARTES: As you say, Socrates, these are very large issues. But I thought we were examining my modest little book, and that book does not raise these issues, but only the issue of my new method for gaining knowledge; it is about the means to knowledge rather than the end of knowledge.

SOCRATES: You are right: we should be returning to your text. But this large detour was not a diversion from it. It placed it into the larger historical context; it put your *tactical* suggestion into the context of a "grand *strategy*", so to speak.

DESCARTES: I claim no strategy as grand as you think, Socrates. I am just a scientist with a new method, a new instrument, a new *Organon*, beyond the old Aristotelian one, as Francis Bacon had also done.

SOCRATES: And to that new instrument we must now turn our attention. Shall we begin by comparing it with the old one?

DESCARTES: Please.

SOCRATES: You and Bacon each seem to have isolated one half of Aristotle's old instrument: Bacon the inductive and sensory half, and you the deductive and purely rational half. So the next two centuries of philosophy after you were destined to be dominated by the issue of epistemology, the philosophical science of knowledge, especially the quest for certainty and the proper method for it; and it would be divided into the two schools that would be called Empiricism and Rationalism. (For some reason, all the important Empiricists were British and all the important Rationalists were continental.)

DESCARTES: And you, Socrates, took the same side in this debate as I did: you were a Rationalist.

SOCRATES: No, not wholly. That is a misunderstanding, and a common one. Aristotle understood me better: he noted that I also invented *inductive* reasoning, which proceeds from an empirical starting point.

DESCARTES: But you were not an Empiricist! An Empiricist is like a worm, blindly crawling through the ground.

SOCRATES: Yes, but is not a mere Rationalist like a cloud, not touching the ground at all? Is it not more complete and more human to be like a tree, with roots in the earth and branches reaching into the heavens?

DESCARTES: You are substituting images for arguments, Socrates. Analogies do not constitute arguments.

SOCRATES: I agree. But images show us things, as the senses do.

DESCARTES: And what your image of the tree shows *me* is that we have been like birds flying over the tree of my philosophy to see "the big picture" but not yet landing in its branches. May we return to the branches of my text, please?

SOCRATES: That is exactly what we should do.

DESCARTES: You keep saying it but not doing it!

SOCRATES: I am justly rebuked. Let's see—we were just up to the point in your text where you say what you derived from the traditional medieval wisdom of philosophy and theology. You say:

> **I revered our theology, and I desired as much as the next man to go to heaven; but having learned as something very certain that the road is no less open to the most ignorant than to the most learned, and that the revealed truths leading to it are beyond our understanding, I would not have dared to subject them to my feeble reasonings. And I believed that, in order to undertake the examination of these truths and to succeed in doing so, it was necessary to have some extraordinary assistance from heaven and to be more than a man.**

DM 1, para. 11

This passage puzzles me for many reasons.

First of all, you speak of having already attained certainty when you say **"having learned as something very certain"**. If "certainty" is your *quest*, why do you say you already had it in your possession?

Second, you say you were taught that **"the road is no less open to the most ignorant than to the most learned"**. Is *that* what you were taught by the best theology teachers in the best school in the world?— that when it comes to theology learning is no better than ignorance, and that knowing the truths revealed from Heaven and properly understanding them does not improve your chances of going to Heaven?

Third, you say you were taught **"that the revealed truths leading to it are beyond our understand-**

ing". If your Jesuit theologians taught you that, they were teaching you that their own science of theology was impossible! For theology is "faith seeking understanding". Did none of these theologians ever distinguish *apprehending* truths about God from *comprehending* them? The second is indeed impossible for a man, as you say, but according to your Scriptures, the first is not only possible but necessary for salvation. (That's in Hebrews 11:6, I think. You can look it up.)

Fourth, you say you **"would not have dared to subject them to my feeble reasonings"**. I wonder why your humility is confined to theology. For in all the other sciences you claim more knowledge and more certainty, not less.

Fifth, you say that to hope to succeed in theology **"it was necessary to have some extraordinary assistance from heaven and to be more than a man"**. So what do you say about the achievement of St. Augustine, from whose treatise *Against the Academics* you borrowed your refutation of skepticism, "I think, therefore I am"? Or of St. Anselm, from whose *Proslogium* you borrowed the ontological argument for the existence of God? What, in fact, do you say about *all* other Christian theologians in history? Do you say of them that they did not succeed, or that they had some extraordinary assistance from Heaven and were more than men? Were they failures or gods? If they were failures, why did you use them? If they were gods, how could gods not know themselves?—for they all said they were *not* gods, and that their theology did *not* come from "some extraordinary assistance from heaven", but that they were using human reason to explore divine revelation.

And, sixth, did you really receive such a poor education in theology that you confused it with religion? For "theology" means only "the science of God", and like any science, it is an abstract, rational discipline, whether it takes its premises from faith in divine revelation or from reason alone. But "religion" is a concrete and personal thing that binds a person with God. (The very word "religion" comes from a Latin word that means "binding".) The purpose of religion is salvation; the purpose of theology is understanding. I cannot believe your teachers were so stupid as to confuse those two things, or that you were. I can only conclude that, if neither you nor your teachers were such dunces, you must have been less than candid in this passage and that you deliberately confused these two things. For this passage cannot stand up under the most elementary examination.

DESCARTES: My book is not about theology but about science and philosophy and their methods. If I have erred in theology, whether by ignorance or deliberately, well, then, I have erred in theology. I accept the judgment of the authorities appointed by God in that matter. But I thought that your job here, Socrates, was only to examine the book of philosophy that I actually wrote, rather than the book of theology that I may have failed to write.

SOCRATES: It was you who brought up the subject of theology in your book, not I. What you have written, you have written, and what you have written, I will question.

DESCARTES: Then I will retract what I have written, if necessary, about theology—but not what I wrote about philosophy. May we examine *that*, please?

SOCRATES: Certainly.

DESCARTES: You must understand my dissatisfaction with the sorry state of philosophy in my time, Socrates. I wrote:

DM 1, para. 12

Of philosophy I shall say only that, aware that philosophy has been cultivated over several centuries by the most excellent minds who have ever lived and that, nevertheless, there is nothing there which is not in some dispute [*dispute*] and thus nothing that is not doubtful [*douteuse*]—I was not so presumptuous as to hope to fare any better.

SOCRATES: **"Nothing there which is not in some dispute and thus nothing that is not doubtful"**— do you recognize the assumption of that argument?

DESCARTES: Of course: that whatever is in dispute is doubtful.

SOCRATES: And you were in search for something that was *not* doubtful, were you not?

DESCARTES: Yes.

SOCRATES: Something like "$2 + 2 = 4$"?

DESCARTES: Yes.

SOCRATES: Suppose I disputed whether 2 + 2 was really 4. Would that make it doubtful?

DESCARTES: Yes, if we assume that whatever is in dispute is doubtful.

SOCRATES: Then I conclude that your search for certainty can never succeed.

DESCARTES: How does that follow?

SOCRATES: Because even if you find a truth that is in itself quite certain, it will become doubtful as soon as one fool chooses to dispute it.

DESCARTES: No, no, that is not what I meant. A proposition that is in itself certain does not become *in itself* uncertain just because one fool disputes it. It only becomes uncertain *to him*.

SOCRATES: Then your assumption that whatever is in dispute is doubtful is not true.

DESCARTES: I suppose it is not.

SOCRATES: Then your argument is worthless, because it depends on that false assumption.

DESCARTES: I retract that argument then.

SOCRATES: So there may be truths that are certain even though they are disputed.

DESCARTES: Yes. But without a method, how can we know what these are?

SOCRATES: Obviously, we cannot, if "a method" means an answer to the question, How can we know them? For there is no way to know without a way to know.

DESCARTES: My point exactly, Socrates. I couldn't have put it better myself.

SOCRATES: But perhaps there are other methods than yours.

DESCARTES: Of course there are! But mine will do what none of the others has ever done.

SOCRATES: And what is that?

DESCARTES: End disagreements. That is what the scientific method has done, and no other method has ever done it.

SOCRATES: This is your central claim, I see. So we must test it. Now there are two ways I know of to test it. One is a rational critique of your arguments for it in your book, which is what we are doing now. The other would be to see, in historical experience, whether it worked in fact, whether philosophers who followed your method agreed more with each other than did the philosophers who followed my method, or Aristotle's method, or whether they agreed *less* with each other. To see whether, centuries later, the term *philosophia perennis*, "the perennial philosophy", the permanent philosophy, the philosophy that lasted and that generated the most agreement—whether this term was used for the new modern philosophy you founded or for the old medieval Scholastic philosophy you sought to replace.

But we are not here for a history lesson; we are here for a lesson in analyzing your text. I will resist the temptation to take another side road, and I will return to your text.

You next mention *three* sources of knowledge and you tell how you moved from one to the other: first, books and tradition, both of which are the fruits of others' experience and thought; then your own experience of the world, acquired through travel; and finally your own thoughts, acquired by turning within, your version of "know thyself":

As soon as age permitted me to escape the tutelage of my teachers, I left the study of letters [books] completely. And resolving to search for no other knowledge than what I could find within myself, or in the great book of the world, I spent the rest of my youth traveling. . . . But after spending many years thus studying in the book of the world and in trying to gain experience, I made up my mind one day also to study myself.

DM 1,
para. 14

DESCARTES: Like you, Socrates. I was climbing up the "divided line" and out of the cave.

SOCRATES: So now let us see where your climb led you, as we begin Part Two of your book.

DESCARTES: Do you plan to linger as long over each of the other Parts as you have over Part One?

SOCRATES: No. I was "priming the pump." Or, to change the metaphor, once we have started to move, we can accelerate.

8

The Reason for the New Method

Let us continue reading from your book:

I was in Germany then, where the wars —
which are still continuing there — called me.
[This was the "Thirty Years' War" (1618–1648),
the bloodiest war so far in history. In some prin-
cipalities it killed one out of every three citizens,
not just soldiers. It was a war of religion, pitting
Protestants against Catholics.] **And while I was
returning to the army from the coronation
of the emperor, the onset of winter held me
up in quarters where, finding no conversation with which to be diverted and, fortunately, otherwise having no worries or passions which troubled me, I remained for a
whole day by myself in a small, stove-heated
room** [what a perfect external symbol for your
mind!], **where I had complete leisure for com-
muning with my thoughts.**

**Among them, one of the first that I thought
of considering was that often there is less
perfection in works made of several pieces
and in works made by the hands of several
masters than in those works on which but
one master has worked. Thus one sees that**

DM 2,
para. 1

buildings undertaken and completed by a single architect are commonly more beautiful and better ordered than those that several architects have tried to patch up, using old walls that had been built for other purposes. Thus those ancient cities that were once merely straggling villages and have become in the course of time great cities are commonly quite poorly laid out, compared to those well-ordered towns that an engineer lays out on a vacant plain as it suits his fancy.

An apt image for a new kind of philosophy: a new kind of city, devoid of chance, tradition, and mystery; a crystal palace of pure reason, all straight lines and straight roads, constructed from scratch by one man, who is almost a second Adam.

DESCARTES: Just as your disciple Plato proposed in his *Republic*. He saw that the just and reasonable state could not come about by a gradual change from traditional regimes, but only by a sudden, complete revolution: if a philosopher became a king or a king became a philosopher. He compared it to dyeing new, white cloth rather than old, already-colored cloth.

SOCRATES: In the centuries after your death, that will be a defining feature of France as distinct from England: revolution in the name of reason as distinct from gradual growth within the limits of tradition. And you make clear your preference for the French way when you say, in the same paragraph,

Thus I imagined that peoples who, having once been half savages and having been civilized only gradually, have made their laws

only to the extent that the inconvenience caused by crimes and quarrels forced them to do so [and that is England's "common-law" tradition, and the Church's procedure too in dealing with heresies as they arise] **would not be as well ordered as those who, from the very beginning of their coming together, have followed the fundamental precepts of some prudent legislator.**

DESCARTES: Yes, and I must remind you that the Church is governed in the French way, not in the English, as I point out next: **"Thus it is quite certain that the state of the true religion, whose ordinances were fixed by God alone, ought to be incomparably better governed than all others."**

SOCRATES: Another side road, and another temptation. But I will not take time to discuss these matters with you now. History has rendered its own verdict on them.

But to continue your story, you clearly summarize your faith in reason over tradition in these words, which almost amount to a formula:

And thus I thought that book learning, at least the kind whose arguments are merely probable and have no demonstrations — having been built up from and enlarged gradually by the opinions of many different people — does not draw as near to the truth as the simple reasonings that can be made naturally by a man of good sense concerning what he encounters (*les simples raisonnements que*

DM 2,
para. 1

*peut faire naturellement un homme de bon sens
touchent les choses qui se présentent).*

DESCARTES: I trust that my faith in reason and in the
common man, rather than in the authority of the so-
called expert, resonates with you, Socrates.

SOCRATES: Oh, it does. I especially love your char-
acterization of the history of philosophy when you
stated that **"having learned since my school days
that one cannot imagine anything so strange or
unbelievable that it has not been said by some
philosopher"**—a saying that characterized the philosophy *after* your time even more than the philosophy
before it. As some will say, of an egregiously absurd
idea, "only a philosopher could believe that."

As for your preference for the common man over
the "experts", this too I share. And that is why I am
puzzled about what you say next, where you seem to
disclaim exactly what you claimed before, and even
to undercut your reason for writing this very book:

**This is why I could not approve of all those
trouble-making types who, called neither by
birth nor by fortune to manage public affairs,
never cease in their imagination to effect
some new reformation.** [That was the really
dangerous word in your time, wasn't it?] **And if
I thought there were the slightest thing in
this essay by means of which one might suspect me of such folly, I would be very sorry
to permit its publication. My plan has never
been more than to reform my own thoughts
and to build upon a foundation which is com-**

DM 2,
para. 3

**pletely my own. And if, my work having suf-
ficiently pleased me, I show it to you here as
a model, it is not for the reason that I wish
to advise anyone to imitate it.**

I have but one question about this passage: Are you
serious?

DESCARTES: What are you suggesting?

SOCRATES: That you meant that passage to be taken
seriously only by your enemies and not by your
friends. That you did not mean it, or believe it, but
said it only to deceive your enemies. That it was a
bone you threw to satisfy the dogs of the Inquisition.
Is this not so?

DESCARTES: And how do you think I would answer
that question if I thought you might be an enemy
instead of a friend?

SOCRATES: Are you doubting my identity now?

DESCARTES: I am having second thoughts, remem-
bering how you toyed with your enemies in Athens.

SOCRATES: If I am the real Socrates, you have no reason to fear me even if I am playful with you. And if I
were a spy for the Inquisition, I would not be playful.

DESCARTES: Ah, but that is just the kind of tricky argument Socrates would use.

SOCRATES: But *not* the dogs of the Inquisition. So
have I convinced you that I am I?

DESCARTES: Let us assume you have.

SOCRATES: In other words, I have not. For if I had, you would not be playing that "let us assume" game with me.

DESCARTES: Socrates, I will be candid, for I seem to be compelled to be candid in this place. I wrote that passage because I did not want to end up as you did. It is not the vocation of every man to be a martyr.

SOCRATES: That is true. But it *is* everyone's vocation to die. And it is often in our power to choose how we die.

DESCARTES: What are you implying?

SOCRATES: You say you are glad you did not end up as I did. But I am glad I did not end up as you did.

DESCARTES: What in the world do you mean by that?

SOCRATES: You died because of the irrational demands of a tyrant, because the Queen of Sweden demanded that you rise so early in the morning to tutor her, all through that dank Swedish winter, that you caught pneumonia and died—like Bacon who died experimenting with refrigeration by stuffing a chicken with snow. Was that a better death than mine or a worse?

DESCARTES: I sense I am being insulted. Do you mean to insult my life by insulting my death?

SOCRATES: Not at all. My aim is not to insult you, but only to ask you to compare yourself with me by comparing your death with mine.

DESCARTES: It was not my vocation to die at the hands of the state.

SOCRATES: Nor was it mine. But we both did, in different ways.

DESCARTES: And it was not my vocation to enter politics.

SOCRATES: Nor was it mine. As I made clear in my *Apology*, I was called by a god to philosophize, and by this god forbidden to enter politics.

DESCARTES: But politics is the point of the passage in my book that you are questioning. And what I wrote there about not planning political reformations was not insincere. As I said, my only reformation was in ideas.

SOCRATES: But ideas have consequences.

DESCARTES: Yes . . .

SOCRATES: And some of them are political.

DESCARTES: *You* should know that, Socrates!

SOCRATES: I was not thinking of the bad consequences of my ideas, my trial and execution, which I did not intend. I was thinking of the good consequences of your ideas. Were these intended?

DESCARTES: In science, certainly.

SOCRATES: No, I mean in politics.

DESCARTES: What good consequences in politics are you thinking of?

SOCRATES: A truly radical one: the abolition of one of mankind's most popular enterprises, and one of the most irrational.

DESCARTES: War, you mean?

SOCRATES: Exactly. Is that not one of the constants of man's history?

DESCARTES: It is.

SOCRATES: And one of the most irrational?

DESCARTES: Many would disagree with that judgment, but I would not. Consider the rationale for war: "Our two nations have a difference of opinion. Since we are rational animals, we can deal with this difference either by our rational powers or by our animal powers, or by both. And if we use both, we could either use our animal powers in the service of reason or use reason to serve our animal powers. So let us do the latter. Let us use our reason to invent ever more powerful weapons to serve our animal rage to kill. Let us deal with our differences of mind by our bodies. Let us solve our problems by killing each other". What a supremely rational invention war is!

SOCRATES: I admire both your reasoning and your satirical powers, René. I too prefer "Come now, let us reason together" to "Come now, let us slaughter together." And I think you claimed to have found a means to this noble end, the abolition of war, that had never been found before—if I am reading your text aright. And I think this is the radical and therefore hidden subtext of your book, between the lines, so to speak.

DESCARTES: Tell me what you see there between my lines, Socrates.

SOCRATES: You hoped to abolish war by discovering its root cause and abolishing *that*. For to take away

106 SOCRATES MEETS DESCARTES

the cause is to take away the effect. But you knew that war has a long and complex chain of causes, so you looked for the first link in that chain. And you found that link in thought, in ideas, in disputes about what was good and evil, just and unjust, true and false. In other words, the origin of war is differences of opinion.

DESCARTES: You have far-seeing eyes, Socrates.

SOCRATES: But this did not take far-seeing eyes on your part. It is easy to see, and not very original. What made you original was your next step. You then looked for the origin of differences of opinion, and you traced this to different *methods* of thinking.

And if this is the cause, it is also the cure. That is why you call for the use of a single method, "the" method. Your method is essentially the scientific method, and if it were to be applied to the most important of the sciences, philosophy, it would end differences of opinion and thus would end wars. For the most ferocious wars stem from divergent philosophies of life, divergent religious philosophies, divergent ethical philosophies, and divergent political philosophies.

DESCARTES: So my *Discourse on Method* was a radical political platform after all—is that your conclusion?

SOCRATES: Did you not admit as much when we spoke of this before?

DESCARTES: I did. For I trusted you. So if you are in fact an inquisitor disguised as a philosopher, you now have sufficient evidence to convict me.

SOCRATES: I assure you, we do not do that sort of thing in this world.

DESCARTES: Then I will candidly admit to you, Socrates, that that was my great hope: that the conquest of passion by reason, which you exemplified so beautifully in *your* life, could be applied to the common life of the common man throughout the world.

SOCRATES: That was also the great hope of the two centuries of thinkers who followed your lead, calling their movement the "Enlightenment", the coming-out from the cave of darkness up into the world of light, the light of reason.

DESCARTES: I am gratified. You have far-seeing eyes indeed: you see into my hope, into my heart. Can you tell me, then, whether my method did in fact bring universal peace to the world?

SOCRATES: I can. But I will not tell you that until you finish explaining your book to me. For I do not want you to interpret your book in light of the future history that you did not know when you wrote it. And if you do not remind me when we finish, I will probably forget it entirely. For my absent-mindedness remains with me even in this world. It seems it is a trait God esteems rather than pities.

9

Who Can Use the New Method?

SOCRATES: Your next passage contains such a blatant
contradiction to what you wrote in your book's very
first paragraph that I cannot believe it was anything
less than deliberate and was a kind of code that only
your disciples would be able to read aright, but not
your enemies. You write here two texts superimposed
on each other like a double exposure in photography
—oh, I'm sorry, I forgot that you lived before that invention—let us say, then, like a palimpsest: one text,
written with visible ink, is for the dogs, and the other,
written with invisible ink, is for the disciples.

DESCARTES: I congratulate you on your perception
again, Socrates. And I deduce that I can trust you
to be a disciple and not a dog. For the dogs are not
bright enough to perceive the contradiction, and thus
they will chew contentedly on the bone I gave them
here, rather than on *my* bones. But my disciples will
find my clue. For I took care to contradict not just
the spirit but even the letter of my first and founda-
tional point, the very first sentence of my book, in
the passage you are now scrutinizing.

SOCRATES: A rather dangerous device, don't you think?
Shouldn't a spy have a less transparent cover?

DESCARTES: I think you overestimate the intelligence of the dogs, Socrates. They chewed your bones to death, after all. But they did not chew mine. My code worked well.

SOCRATES: Well, here is the passage. Let us call it "the bone":

The single resolution to detach oneself from all the beliefs one has once accepted as true [you here refer to the first and most important step of your method, namely, universal methodic doubt] **is not an example that everyone ought to follow; and the world consists almost completely of but two kinds of people, and for these two kinds it is not at all suitable: namely (1) those who, believing themselves more capable than they really are, cannot help making premature judgments and do not have enough patience to conduct their thoughts in an orderly manner. . . . (2) Now as for those people who have enough reason or modesty to judge that they are less capable to distinguish the true from the false than are others by whom they can be instructed, they ought to content themselves more with following the opinions of these others than to look for better opinions on their own.**

DM 2, para. 3

In the very first sentence of your book you claimed that reason (which you identified with common sense, or "good sense", or **"the ability to distinguish the true from the false"**) was common to all and equal in all. Yet here you say that some men have less of this capability than others do.

Also, in the very first paragraph of your book you claimed that all men are satisfied with the amount of "good sense" they have, and that **"it is unlikely that anyone is mistaken about that."** So the second class of people in "the bone" passage simply does not exist according to your first paragraph: the class of people who have the **"modesty to judge that they are *less* capable to distinguish the true from the false than are others"**. That describes *my* attitude. So since that class of people includes me, and since you say that that class of people does not exist, you are telling me that I do not exist. To whom are you talking now, then? It is wonderful to dialogue with the dead, but why dialogue with the nonexistent? You will later prove your own existence, by your famous "I think, therefore I am", but you deny mine.

DESCARTES: Are you joking or are you serious?

SOCRATES: May a man not be both? However, my serious point is that you seem to write as two different people. In your first paragraph you are modern, egalitarian, and optimistic about man's reason and about his estimation of his own reason; but in "the bone" you are premodern, aristocratic, and pessimistic about both the quantity of reason in most men and about the accuracy of their self-estimate— just as Plato was. Surely one cannot take both passages seriously.

DESCARTES: Unless you are a dog looking for a bone.

SOCRATES: I understand. So let us return, as disciples rather than dogs, to your program for enlightenment. You are explaining why you felt the need for a new method by telling us your dissatisfaction with the results of the old ones; and that dissatisfaction, in one word, was "uncertainty", or "doubt". You were very sensitive to this because your age, like mine, was one of decreasing provincialism and increasing contact with other cultures, with the natural result of a skepticism and cultural relativism. Thus you say:

Having learned since my school days that one cannot imagine anything so strange or unbelievable that it has not been said by some philosopher, and since then, during my travels, having acknowledged that those who have feelings quite contrary to our own are not for that reason barbarians or savages, but that many of them use their reason as much or more than we do, and having considered how the very same man with his very own mind, having been brought up from infancy among the French or the Germans becomes different from what he would be had he always lived among the Chinese or among cannibals [by the way, I notice that another edition of your text has, instead of "cannibals", "Americans"!], **and how, even to the fashions of our clothing, the same thing that pleased us ten years ago and that perhaps might again please us ten years from now seems to us extravagant and ridiculous. Thus it is more custom and ex-**

DM 2, para. 4

ample that persuades us than certain knowledge.

But was there not a method already in place for
judging between different opinions and customs, and
transforming mere opinion into certainty through
demonstration? I mean the method of logic. It had
been known and used for two thousand years, and I
thought I had a little to do with that. And Aristotle had systematized the rules of this method that I
had discovered and used, in his *Organon*, the world's
first logic textbook. What was wrong with that as a
method for attaining certainty?

DESCARTES: Oh, I am very grateful to you and Aristotle for your valuable example and for his valuable
principles. But, as I wrote next, **"I saw that in the
case of logic, its syllogisms and the greater part of
its other lessons served more to explain to someone else what one knows . . . than to learn them."**

SOCRATES: If you were looking for a logic for learning new truths, why didn't you use Bacon's new inductive logic text, the *New Organon*?

DESCARTES: Because I found the same problem in it
as I did in your deductive logic: the problem of com-
plexity. I do not accuse either Aristotle or Bacon of
theoretical error but of a practical defect; as I wrote,

**Since the multiplicity of laws often provides
excuses for vices, so that a state is much better when, having but a few laws, its laws are**
DM 2,   **strictly observed; so, in place of the large**
para. 6   **number of rules of which logic is composed,**

I believed that the following four rules would be sufficient, provided I made a firm and constant resolution not even once to fail to observe them. . . .

SOCRATES: So we come here at last to the heart of your book: the scientific method in its barest essentials, its most general principles.

DESCARTES: Exactly. And my subsequent chapters apply this method, first to morality, in chapter 3, then to philosophy, in chapter 4, then to theoretical physics, in chapter 5, and then to applied physics, or technology, in chapter 6.

10

The Method Itself

DESCARTES: Here, then, are the four rules of the method:

DM 2,
para. 7

[1a] **The first was never to accept anything as true that I did not know evidently to be such; that is, carefully to avoid precipitous judgment and prejudice;**
[1b] **and to include nothing more in my judgments than what presented itself to my mind with such clarity and distinctness that I would have no occasion to put it in doubt;**

DM 2,
para. 8

[2] **The second, to divide each of the difficulties I was examining into as many parts as possible and as is required to solve them best.**

DM 2,
para. 9

[3] **The third, to conduct my thoughts in an orderly fashion, commencing with the simplest and easiest to know objects, to rise gradually, as by degrees, to the knowledge of the most composite things, and even supposing an order among those things that do not naturally precede one another.**

DM 2,
para. 10

[4] **And last, everywhere to make enumerations so complete and reviews so general**

that I would be sure of having omitted nothing.

SOCRATES: These four rules seem very practical and commonsensical. *When* do you think we should use them?

DESCARTES: Whenever we want to do scientific thinking about anything. Like the syllogistic logic you used, they can be used for an infinite variety of contents. They are a universal form for thinking if the thinking is to be scientific in the most basic and general sense.

SOCRATES: I see. And do you believe that philosophical thinking should be scientific in this most basic and general sense?

DESCARTES: Of course. That is one of the main reasons I gave my method to the world.

SOCRATES: And you claim that your new method can teach you how to acquire new knowledge?

DESCARTES: Yes.

SOCRATES: And that the old method, Aristotle's logic, could not do that?

DESCARTES: Yes.

SOCRATES: So you say a syllogism cannot teach you new knowledge but only explain something already known?

DESCARTES: I am not attacking deductive reasoning itself. Far from it. But I say that the syllogism is far less useful for discovering truth than the Scholastic philosophers thought. And the reason I say this is that the truth of the conclusion is already logically implied in the truth of the premises if the argument is logically valid.

SOCRATES: Do you think it is possible that you might know that both premises are true and also that the conclusion is true, but not know that the premises are the reason for the conclusion? For instance, suppose you know that someone hates you, but you wonder why. You also know that you are much more intelligent than he is. Then a mutual friend tells you that he hates you because of envy. That might be new knowledge to you, might it not?

DESCARTES: Yes indeed.

SOCRATES: But your friend explained this relationship by means of a syllogism, or at least an enthymeme, a syllogism with one implied premise, which you also already knew, namely that those who envy, hate the object of their envy.

DESCARTES: That is so.

SOCRATES: And in that case, did not a syllogism teach you *that* new knowledge?

DESCARTES: I suppose you could call that new knowledge—a knowledge, not of a new truth, but of a new causal relationship between two truths. But the truth of the conclusion of the syllogism was already known.

SOCRATES: But isn't it also possible that one may know both premises but never put them together in his mind and draw the conclusion? In that case, the truth of the conclusion would be new knowledge to him. And it was brought about by the syllogism.

DESCARTES: Can you give me an example of this in philosophical or theoretical knowledge?

SOCRATES: I think I have an excellent example in a book that is somewhere around here—I seem to have misplaced it. . . .

DESCARTES: Some esoteric book by some arcane philosopher, no doubt.

SOCRATES: The philosopher is named René Descartes and the book is called *Discourse on Method*.

DESCARTES: Oh.

SOCRATES: Ah, here is the book. And here are the two premises that you already clearly know, or believe. The first is that *all* good philosophical thinking should follow your scientific method. And the second is that the method itself is the first part of good philosophical thinking. Do you see what logically follows from these two premises? Or have you never put these two premises together until this moment and drawn the logical conclusion from them that now seems to embarrass you (for I notice that your face has become slightly red), namely, that your method itself must be tested by your method.

DESCARTES: Touché. That was tricky, Socrates.

SOCRATES: Surely you do not call logical consistency a trick?

DESCARTES: No.

SOCRATES: Surely you do not fear that your method would *fail* such a test, do you?—that the method which you claim is the distilled essence of the scientific method should be proved to be unscientific? And by means of the method itself? Surely you do not fear that your whole philosophy is based on that self-contradictory assumption?

DESCARTES: Indeed not!

SOCRATES: Good. Then you have nothing to fear from my examination of your method itself.

DESCARTES: I do not. But by what standard do you propose to evaluate my method, Socrates?

SOCRATES: Why, by the standards of the method itself, of course. Do you think there is a fairer standard than that?

DESCARTES: No.

SOCRATES: Or do you think perhaps that there is a *better* standard in some way, a *higher* standard?

DESCARTES: No, not for scientific thinking . . . but . . .

SOCRATES: Why do you hesitate?

DESCARTES: Because if you are demanding that my method prove itself, I say that that is an impossible demand, just as it is impossible for your syllogisms either to prove their own rules, or to prove their own premises. For that would be the fallacy of "begging the question", assuming what you must prove.

SOCRATES: I quite agree with you.

DESCARTES: Oh.

SOCRATES: Did you think I was deficient in logic? I virtually invented it, you know.

DESCARTES: So you do not demand that my method prove itself.

SOCRATES: Of course not. Only that it not contradict itself.

DESCARTES: Oh. Well, I have no fear of that.

SOCRATES: Then you have no fear of me.

DESCARTES: I do believe that.

SOCRATES: So we both accept the principle that you cannot prove the validity of anything by assuming that very thing, whether it is your method, or my syllogisms, or anything else.

DESCARTES: Yes.

SOCRATES: Then we cannot prove the validity of human reason itself by means of some act of human reason, for that act would assume the validity of human reason.

DESCARTES: That follows from our principle.

SOCRATES: So that is *not* the purpose of your method, then? I mean, to place everything in doubt, even human reason itself; to demand critical proof of our very mental tools before we go on to build our idea-houses with them; and then, having demanded critical proof of its validity, to supply it.

DESCARTES: That would be impossible, for it is self-contradictory. How could one of the prisoners on trial be the judge of the innocence of all the prisoners? Once *all* acts of reasoning are put on trial, no *one* act of reasoning can judge and exonerate itself and all the rest.

SOCRATES: I am glad to see that you do not fall into that fallacy, as some of your critics claim you do. They say you were the first to raise the "critical problem" of a "critique of reason" itself. Others praise you for raising this new question rather than blaming you for it.

DESCARTES: I deny deserving either the blame or the praise. Perhaps others had such lofty and impossible ambitions, but mine were more modest.

SOCRATES: Then let us return to your more modest method and ask what does justify it, if it does not justify itself. Surely it is not arbitrary. Surely you can give a good reason for it.

DESCARTES: Of course.

SOCRATES: I think you can guess my next question.

DESCARTES: My answer is as obvious as your question, Socrates. It is utility. A method is justified by its results. A method is not a house but a tool, not a science but an instrument, not a set of indicatives but a set of imperatives. I do not need to prove it to be *true*, for it does not make claims to be true, only to be *useful*.

SOCRATES: Useful for what end?

DESCARTES: Useful for finding truth—and finding it with certainty. That is its superiority over all other methods. I admit there are many methods of finding truth, but mine yields certainty and therefore can hope to overcome differences of opinions, as I said before.

SOCRATES: Certainty about what? Differences of opinion about what?

DESCARTES: About anything! I was thinking of the wonderful exhibition of teaching geometry that you yourself gave to Meno's slave boy when I wrote the following passage:

> **Those long chains of reasoning, each of them simple and easy, that geometricians commonly use to attain their most difficult demonstrations, have given me an occasion for imagining that all the things that can fall within human knowledge follow one another in the same way** [that is, deductively] **and that, provided only that one abstain from accepting anything as true that is not true, and that one always maintains the order to be followed in deducing the one from the other, there is nothing so far distant that one cannot finally reach nor so hidden that one cannot discover.**

DM 2,
para. 11

SOCRATES: Nothing, René? Nothing at all?

DESCARTES: Nothing in this finite universe. I do not speak of the mysteries of God, of course.

SOCRATES: So for everything in the universe you would say that if it is real it is rational, and if it is rational we can know it, if only we use your method properly, so therefore everything in the universe is knowable by your method?

DESCARTES: That is a valid syllogism, Socrates, and all of its propositions are true. Yes, everything in the universe is knowable in principle by my method.

SOCRATES: And by "knowable" you mean "discoverable"?

DESCARTES: Yes.

SOCRATES: And also "comprehensible"?

DESCARTES: Yes.

SOCRATES: And also "provable"?

DESCARTES: Yes.

SOCRATES: With certainty?

DESCARTES: Yes.

SOCRATES: That is an amazing claim.

DESCARTES: If you find it hard to believe, there is only one thing necessary to disprove it: to produce one truth that is *not* discoverable, or one concept that is *not* comprehensible, or one conclusion that is *not* provable, ever, by reason properly used.

SOCRATES: But is that not an impossible demand to fulfill? For if anyone *should* produce one truth that he claims is not discoverable, the act of producing it would dis-cover it. And if anyone should produce a concept that he claims is not comprehensible, the act of producing it would comprehend it, for otherwise it would not be a concept at all but only a meaningless sound. And if anyone should produce a true conclusion that he claims cannot be proved, he must believe that conclusion to be true, and he must have some reasons to believe that it is true, and those reasons are the premises that prove that conclusion.

You see, reason cannot, in principle, produce something irrational. For whatever reason produces is rational. Reason cannot produce something that reason cannot produce. That would be a self-contradiction. So your statement that this cannot be done is a tautology: it is true by its logical form alone quite irrespective of content.

DESCARTES: It may be a tautology, but it is still true.

SOCRATES: But it does not validate your method. That all things in the universe are in principle rational—knowable in principle by reason—that may be not only true but also a tautology. But that all things are knowable *by this method* of yours rather than by some other, and that no things escape your method—that is not a tautology, and has not yet been proved to be true. You are so far only a salesman with a promise.

DESCARTES: That is so. But my promise will be fulfilled.

SOCRATES: How?

DESCARTES: By practice. A practical claim is fulfilled in practice, and my claim for my method is a practical claim, therefore it will be fulfilled in practice, by the success of the method when used. It is not fair for you or anyone else to demand a theoretical justification for a practical thing.

SOCRATES: That is true. But on the other hand, there should be no logical contradiction in the practical method either, don't you agree?

DESCARTES: Of course. Do you think you see one?

SOCRATES: Perhaps. Let us look more carefully. Do you say that your method is something knowable?

DESCARTES: Of course. How else could I teach it?

SOCRATES: But you have already admitted that the method cannot prove itself.

DESCARTES: Yes.

SOCRATES: Then it follows that not everything knowable can be proved by the method!

DESCARTES: Oh. Well, then, I will escape the self-contradiction by moderating my claim. All *other* things can be proved by the method. It is like the sun: it cannot be illumined by the sun, by itself; but everything else can.

SOCRATES: That does escape self-contradiction. But I think I may see another self-contradiction in the first of the four specific points of your method, in accepting only clear and distinct ideas as certainly true. For that point itself does not seem to be a clear and distinct idea.

The other steps of your method are not thus self-contradictory. To use division and analysis does not itself violate the rule of division and analysis. To proceed in order from simple to complex is itself orderly and simple. And there is no contradiction in subjecting to a universal review your entire philosophy, including the method, including this fourth point of the method, the demand for a universal review. But the first step, to treat everything as false until it is proved true, to begin with universal doubt—this does seem to be self-contradictory. For it can be doubted, and it was, in fact, by not just a few philosophers but almost all of them who came before you! Yet you do not doubt that we should begin with doubt. The contradiction is this: you claim your doubt is universal, but it is not: it does not doubt itself. You do not doubt either the fact that you are doubting or the rightness of doing so.

DESCARTES: Well, then, I shall avoid this self-contradiction by modifying the universality of my doubt just as I modified the universality of my claim for the power of the method. It doesn't matter, for the method still works practically. It works wonderfully well for everything except itself.

SOCRATES: So you still claim that there are no real things, or no truths about real things, that cannot be known by the method?

DESCARTES: That is what I claim.

SOCRATES: Or that cannot be known better by another method?

DESCARTES: I did not say that.

SOCRATES: Do you say there is a better method for knowing some things than yours, then, or not?

DESCARTES: Let us suppose I say there is not.

SOCRATES: Do you say that there is anything that is better known by not doubting than by doubting?

DESCARTES: Not at the beginning. Doubt is the best beginning. The purpose of beginning with doubt is to end with certainty. I hope you understand that my universal doubt does not make me a skeptic. Far from it. But I am not a dogmatist either. I do not *begin* with certainty, I only hope to *end* with it. For I believe that if we begin with certainty, we shall end with doubt, while if we begin with doubt we may end with certainty.

SOCRATES: And is this true about everything in the universe?

DESCARTES: Yes.

SOCRATES: Are *you* something in the universe?

DESCARTES: Yes.

SOCRATES: Then you too must be known best by beginning with doubting you rather than trusting you. But is this so? Can I understand you best by doubting you rather than by trusting you? Are people known better by doubting everything about them, including their very existence and the truth of all their words, until you have proven these things to be true?

DESCARTES: Obviously not. I speak not of knowing people, Socrates, only of knowing ideas. People should be treated as innocent until proved guilty, but ideas should be treated as guilty until proved innocent, false until proved true.

SOCRATES: All ideas? Are all the ideas in all the minds of all people at all times and in all situations best known by treating them as you would treat a hypothesis in science?

DESCARTES: Of course not, Socrates. I am not suggesting that everyone use my method at all times. We would never learn anything if we began by disbelieving all our teachers, or if we began as infants by disbelieving the testimony of our senses. This method is only for science and philosophy.

SOCRATES: So it presupposes that we have already learned by trusting our senses and our parents and teachers, as all children learn.

DESCARTES: Of course.

SOCRATES: And that is faith, rather than doubt.

DESCARTES: Among children? Yes.

SOCRATES: So your method of doubt really presupposes faith.

DESCARTES: No, no, it does not *presuppose* faith, as a premise. It has no premises.

SOCRATES: It may not *logically* presuppose faith, but it does *really* presuppose faith. For if someone never had had any faith in his senses and his teachers, he could never use your method. Without the steps of faith, he cannot take the steps of doubt.

DESCARTES: Well, of course. But those steps of faith are not part of *the method*; they are only part of the early history of the person who grows up to use it.

SOCRATES: Would you agree, then, that your scientific method is *not* like the principles of mathematics but more like the practical principles of surgery or military defense? Let me explain what I mean by that distinction. The principles of mathematics are changeless, abstract, and self-sufficient, but the principles of surgery and military defense are needed and heeded by us only because we are prone to error and ignorance, weakness and danger.

DESCARTES: If I understand your distinction correctly, then I agree the method is like a method of surgery or war. It is practical.

SOCRATES: Does it follow, then, that the reason it is useful for mankind is something like the reason surgery and military defense are useful?

DESCARTES: Yes.

SOCRATES: And when are they useful? Do we find surgery useful when we are healthy?

DESCARTES: No, when we are ill.

SOCRATES: And do we find armies and navies useful when we are at peace?

DESCARTES: No, when we are at war.

SOCRATES: So when do we find such practical things useful?

DESCARTES: When we are in need.

SOCRATES: Real needs or only felt needs?

DESCARTES: Real needs. For we may be mistaken about our needs.

SOCRATES: Quite so. And are we in need of these things all the time?

DESCARTES: No, only in some situations.

SOCRATES: Some real situations?

DESCARTES: Of course. Why do you ask that?

SOCRATES: Because the first step of your method is to doubt *everything* that seems to be real, including the whole situation and its needs. In fact, you doubt the whole world.

DESCARTES: True.

SOCRATES: Do you not see an apparent contradiction?

DESCARTES: Not at all. I see a self-contradiction in universal *skepticism* as a philosophy—how can you know that you cannot know—but not in universal doubt as a method. My advice to doubt the whole world is not skepticism; it is the way to *refute* skepticism. It is for the sake of knowing the whole world more certainly. It is like a child leaving his parents and his family upon reaching adulthood: his leaving his family is for the sake of a better, more adult relationship with his family later on. Is not that a reasonable analogy?

SOCRATES: It seems to be. But rather than pressing this question further now, I have another question.

DESCARTES: Why am I not surprised at that?

SOCRATES: It is this: is it reasonable to speak of "the" method, of a single method for certainty in everything? For finding a lost coin, for detecting invisible waves of energy, for grading a language test, for solving an equation in algebra, for getting to Lithuania, and for getting to Heaven?

DESCARTES: Why not? Surely there is something common to all these problems, namely their logical form.

SOCRATES: And there is also something that differentiates them, and that something is their material content. But different content, or matter, would seem to require different methods. Do you deny that common-sense principle?

DESCARTES: Not at all. I do not claim that my method is the only one to use, by anyone, ever. I only say that it is the most scientific method, and the best one to use in finding certainty in any of the sciences.

SOCRATES: So you do not deny that there are some things that are better known by *not* using your method, especially not using the first step of your method, universal doubt and the insistence on what you call "clear and distinct" ideas?

DESCARTES: I do not deny that. I know that when it is a matter of knowing people, as distinct from ideas, it is trust rather than mistrust that is often necessary. I would also say that the insistence on clear and distinct ideas can also be a hindrance in knowing people, at least at first. Also, my advice to use analysis before synthesis is not appropriate for knowing people, for one's intuitive first impression sometimes reveals what analysis cannot reveal. And there is another rule in my method that is often better to disobey rather than to obey when it comes to knowing people: I say to begin with the simple and proceed to the complex, but it is often best to begin with the complex whole that is the person rather than with one simple and easier-to-know aspect or part or dimension of the person, such as his age or name or intelligence. No, my method is not designed for everyday life, but for the sciences.

SOCRATES: Is philosophy a science?

DESCARTES: Indeed it is.

SOCRATES: And are all men called to philosophize?

DESCARTES: No, for not all are called to be scientific.

SOCRATES: But are not all men called to be wise?

DESCARTES: Yes.

SOCRATES: And is not philosophy the love of wisdom?

DESCARTES: Yes.

SOCRATES: Then all men are called to philosophize —as you yourself explained at the beginning of your book, where you appealed to a **"reason"** that was so common that you called it **"mankind's most equally distributed endowment"**. In fact, you denied that there are any inherent differences between men in their ability to judge between the true and the false.

DESCARTES: Perhaps there are three different kinds of philosophy: the kind of philosophy all men are called to, which is your kind; the kind of philosophy that is only for those who wish to think scientifically, like myself; and the fake kind of philosophy that I found in my day in the late medieval Schools, the kind that is pseudo-scientific, that has neither the popular appeal and intelligibility your philosophy had, nor the truly scientific method and certainty that my philosophy has. You see, Socrates, I studied this Scholastic philosophy, in the best schools in the world, and it was so technical and difficult that very few men could understand it. That is why I sought a simpler method, one that all men could use when thinking critically—as you did too, Socrates. You too found a method everyone could follow: the syllogism.

SOCRATES: But when I read your more thoroughly philosophical book, the *Meditations*, I find myself in the presence of concepts so abstract, and arguments so difficult, that few ordinary people could understand them—unlike my dialogues. I argued with soldiers and playboys and sophists, and I myself was a stone cutter. And they all understood me. Do you think they could understand you?

DESCARTES: Probably not.

SOCRATES: Then you are closer to the very technical, Scholastic philosophy that you rejected, than to my kind of philosophy.

DESCARTES: Alas, that was the opposite of my intention and my goal.

SOCRATES: Then your method did not attain your goal. And what method was that, again? Isn't there a book about it somewhere around here?

II

Descartes' Mathematicism

SOCRATES: Before we explore your third chapter, which contains four moral principles, there is one other matter I should like to question. You say that

there being but one truth for each thing, anyone who finds it knows as much as one can know about that thing. . . . For example, a child given lessons in arithmetic, having made one addition in accordance with its rules, can be assured of having found everything the human mind can find bearing on the sum he has examined.

DM 2,
para. 12

I grant you that the method used in the mathematical sciences does yield this result, but do you say that this method will yield the same result in the other sciences and even in philosophy? If so, I have some questions about this claim. If not, what is the point of your example from arithmetic, if not to exemplify a more general principle?

DESCARTES: I do claim that, Socrates. And I am surprised that you question it. Surely every proposition is either true or false, whether its content is numbers or anything else; and we either know that this is true or we do not. What do you question?

SOCRATES: I question whether this is the only thing you mean by "know"?

DESCARTES: I suppose you could use the word "know" to refer to modes of awareness that are not scientific, not methodological, not logical—an intuitive sense, for instance. But I would not call that "knowledge".

SOCRATES: But about scientific knowledge that proceeds by strict logical method—do you claim that all such knowledge falls under your principle?

DESCARTES: I do.

SOCRATES: So do you mean to say that when you know that all men are mortal, and a five-year-old child also knows that all men are mortal, the two of you know exactly the same thing?

DESCARTES: Indeed.

SOCRATES: And that you do not know more than he does?

DESCARTES: That is exactly what I say.

SOCRATES: Because both of you know the simple fact that it is true that all men are mortal?

DESCARTES: Yes. You see my point, Socrates. What is there to question in it?

SOCRATES: Do you not *understand what you mean* more than the child does? Do you not have a clearer and more adequate concept of "man" and of "mortal" than he has?

DESCARTES: Yes, of course.

SOCRATES: But you say you *know* no more than the child does.

DESCARTES: Yes.

SOCRATES: Then you must not classify that as "knowledge".

DESCARTES: Classify *what* as knowledge?

SOCRATES: Knowing exactly what you mean by your terms when you utter a proposition.

DESCARTES: That's right.

SOCRATES: But I think most people *would* call that "knowledge". And here is a second thing most people would call "knowledge" that you apparently do not call "knowledge": when you "know" that all men are mortal, you also know *why* this is so, and that it *must* be so. But a child may not know the reason, the why: that it is because an animal body is part of human nature. And even when he does, he may think, wrongly, that this is not necessary but accidental and changeable, like the fact that all men so far have been less than twelve feet tall. But would you not call these two things—knowing-the-reason-why and knowing-the-necessity—would you not call these things "knowledge"?

DESCARTES: I see your point, Socrates. I was speaking only of judgment, the second act of the mind. You are speaking of understanding and also of reasoning, the first and third acts of the mind. If you want to call these two things "knowledge", and I do not, that is only a matter of the use of words.

SOCRATES: But when you use the word "know" in that passage I quoted, saying that there is nothing more in a proposition for an adult to "know" than a child, you then mislead your audience if you do not use the word "know" in the same way they do.

DESCARTES: But I was speaking only of mathematical equations. And there, it is as I say. A child knows that $2 + 2 = 4$, and so does an adult, and there is no difference there.

SOCRATES: But there *is* a difference when we speak of man and mortality and virtue and such things rather than about numbers, is there not?

DESCARTES: I admit that.

SOCRATES: But isn't the point you are making here that the mathematical method is applicable to all things? Didn't you just say a page earlier that the long chains of reasoning that the geometers use may be applied to all things knowable and that there is nothing so distant or hidden that we cannot discover it by this method? That would seem to be a rather radical claim, not merely a matter of how we choose to use words to say what we all already knew to be true.

DESCARTES: Yes, that is my point: that the mathematical method is applicable to all things.

SOCRATES: Surely you understand that most people would disagree with this claim.

DESCARTES: Yes.

SOCRATES: And surely you have an answer ready to their objections to it.

DESCARTES: Which objections? If they give reasons, I shall answer them. If they merely utter prejudices, I cannot refute them.

SOCRATES: Well, suppose they gave this reason. Suppose they say that mathematical knowledge can attain a certainty that other knowledge cannot attain only because of its unique content: numbers. For numbers are exactly distinguished from each other, and they are the only language that is utterly unambiguous, and they can be understood by small children as well as by adults. But when we speak of real things like human nature, and animal nature, and the virtues, these things are not distinguished from each other as twoness and threeness, and they are not utterly unambiguous, and they are certainly not knowable as well by small children as by wise adults.

DESCARTES: Perhaps that is only because no one has tried to use the mathematical method on them. Whether my thought experiment is successful or not cannot be determined a priori, before we attempt to do it. The proof of the pudding is in the eating. No matter how radical my proposal seems, and no matter how much it contradicts ordinary opinions, it must be proved or disproved by testing. Do you not agree with that principle?

SOCRATES: I do.

DESCARTES: Then let us return to the testing, and to my book.

SOCRATES: Let us do exactly that, and look briefly at Part Three of your book.

12

Descartes' Provisional Morality

SOCRATES: In Part Three, you give us four practical rules to live by. I will read what I think is a summary of your description of their purpose, and then your four rules. Please tell me if you think I have omitted anything essential.

Now just as it is not enough, before beginning to rebuild the house where one lives, to pull it down, to make provisions for materials and architects, or to take a try at architecture for oneself, and also to have carefully worked out the floor plan; one must provide for something else in addition, namely where one can be conveniently sheltered while working on the other building; so too, in order not to remain irresolute in my actions while reason requires me to be so in my judgments, and in order not to cease living during that time as happily as possible, I formulated a provisional code of morals, which consisted of but three or four maxims. . . .

The first was to obey the laws and the customs of my country, firmly holding on

DM 3, para. 1

DM 3, para. 2

138

to the religion in which, by God's grace, I was instructed from childhood, and governing myself in all other things according to the most moderate opinions and . . . to follow the opinions of those who were the most sensible. . . .

My second maxim was to be as firm and resolute in my actions as I could be, and to follow with no less constancy the most doubtful opinions, once I have decided upon them, than if they were very certain. In this way I would imitate travelers who, finding themselves lost in a forest, ought not wander this way and that . . . but walk as straight a line as they can in one direction and not change course for feeble reasons. . . .

DM 3, para. 3

My third maxim was always to try to conquer myself rather than fortune, to change my desires rather than the order of the world; and generally to become accustomed to believing that there is nothing that is utterly within our power except for our thoughts. . . .

DM 3, para. 4

Finally, to conclude this code of morals, I thought it advisable to review the various occupations that men take up in this life, so as to try to choose the best one . . .

DM 3, para. 5

DESCARTES: That is indeed a fair summary. What do you want to know about it?

SOCRATES: Whether you believed it.

DESCARTES: Do you think I was *lying*?

SOCRATES: No, but I wonder whether this was another bone you threw to the censors.

DESCARTES: Of course it was. These principles are not radical, as my new system of thought was. But that does not mean I lied. I stand by these four maxims.

SOCRATES: Do you claim they are true?

DESCARTES: No, nor are they false. They are not theoretical but practical.

SOCRATES: I see. Then they are not certain but probable.

DESCARTES: Correct.

SOCRATES: And not final but provisional.

DESCARTES: Correct again. That is how I described them. Remember my image of building the house. You must exist, and live, and survive, and be sheltered while you are building this new house. And I had to live while I was building my new system of thought. And I could not yet live according to the new system, but only according to the old one. That is why the old one seems to contradict the new one.

SOCRATES: The attentive reader would surely spot a contradiction between these four maxims and the four rules of your method, especially the first of the four. For the first rule of your method is to doubt all received, traditional opinions, while the first rule of your morality is to accept them without doubt and live by them.

DESCARTES: Of course. For there is a great difference between how to live in the little shack one inhabits while constructing a mansion, and how to live in the mansion.

SOCRATES: And when you do build the mansion, will you be able to live in it?

DESCARTES: Of course.

SOCRATES: So the mansion—your new system of thought—is not merely a work of art to be held up and contemplated, but a house to live in?

DESCARTES: Indeed. In fact, it will bring about a better life: progress and peace and happiness on earth, and not merely in thought.

SOCRATES: Two centuries after your death, another philosopher will make a claim similar to yours and construct a very rational system similar to yours. His name is Hegel. And he will have a critic very similar to your critic Pascal, who criticized your system as being "useless and uncertain". His critic's name is Kierkegaard. And his criticism is essentially that the rational system of thought that Hegel constructed is like a castle without doors. One can contemplate it in wonder but one cannot live in it. One can live only in the little shack outside its walls, as you can live only in the so-called provisional maxims that you hope some day to transcend when you apply your new method to the questions of morality and construct a wholly rational system of ethics. Such a system may be thinkable but not livable—that will be the essential critique of the whole movement of thought called the "Enlightenment" that you fathered.

DESCARTES: How very interesting. But what is your question, Socrates?

SOCRATES: I understand that this set of moral maxims was not intended to be certain or even, by the strict standards of your new method, rational. Did you hope eventually to construct such a system of ethics on the basis of your new method?

DESCARTES: I did. But I never got around to it. I died too soon.

SOCRATES: It would interest you, then, to know that there is another man, now waiting in line to get into this place, who claims to have done exactly that. His name is Immanuel Kant, and his book *Foundations of the Metaphysics of Morals* is on my list to examine soon. You might want to be an invisible "fly on the wall" and overhear that conversation when it happens.

DESCARTES: Nothing would fascinate me more, Socrates. Thank you.

SOCRATES: But first we must finish your book. And that means the summary of your new system of philosophy in Part Four. All that we have said before that Part is preliminary—a rather long preliminary, I admit—and all that we will say after that Part, in investigating the claims you make for the other sciences in Parts Five and Six, can be very short. So we are now ready for the main course.

DESCARTES: My appetite is keen, Socrates.

SOCRATES: That is good, but it is not enough. I hope your food is also digestible.

13

Step One of Descartes' Philosophical System: Universal Doubt

SOCRATES: Since your thought is ordered in a linear way, from one point to another as from premise to conclusion, I think it will be best if we divide your philosophical system, as summarized here, into six stages:

First, your methodological starting point of universal doubt.

Second, your first certainty, the "I think, therefore I am", your "Archimedean point".

Third, your anthropology, your answer to the question *what* you are.

Fourth, your epistemology, especially your criterion for truth, "clear and distinct ideas".

Fifth, your metaphysics or philosophical theology, your proofs for the existence of God.

Sixth, your philosophical foundation for the sciences, your proof for the reality of the physical world.

So we begin at the beginning.

DESCARTES: And my beginning is the only beginning that is unquestionable.

SOCRATES: I wonder whether there is anything at all that is unquestionable.

DESCARTES: As history's great questioner, you should be the touchstone for that.

SOCRATES: Then please touch your "unquestionable" new beginning to this "stone" that is myself. Tell me what is so totally new in your beginning and why it is unquestionable.

DESCARTES: I can answer both questions at once. What is totally new is that I begin with nothing at all: with no assumptions, no premises. And if there are no assumptions, there can be no questionable assumptions.

SOCRATES: It is certainly true that if there are no assumptions, there can be no questionable assumptions. It only remains to be seen whether you do indeed begin with nothing, as you say.

DESCARTES: Do you think I have some hidden assumption that I am hiding? How could you show such a thing?

SOCRATES: No, I do not think you are hiding anything.

DESCARTES: Then what might be questionable in my making everything questionable?

SOCRATES: Perhaps the *act* of making everything questionable.

DESCARTES: But this is purely practical. It is not a hidden assumption, or a premise. It is merely a method, not a way of life—a thought experiment, if you like.

SOCRATES: I understand that. But even with a mere thought-experiment, the experimenter cannot be part of the experiment. The thinker cannot be merely one of his thoughts.

DESCARTES: True. But I do not see how that fact casts doubt upon my method of beginning with universal doubt.

SOCRATES: Let us first look in detail at your new beginning, your "universal methodic doubt"; then we will see whether your doubt is as universal as it claims to be.

Here is the text, the beginning of Part Four of your book:

I do not know whether I ought to tell you about the first meditations I made there; for they are so metaphysical and so out of the ordinary, that perhaps they would not be to everyone's liking. Nevertheless, so that one might be able to judge whether the foundations I have laid are sufficiently firm, I am in some sense forced to speak.

DM 4, para. 1

For a long time I have noticed that in moral matters one must sometimes follow opinions that one knows are quite uncertain, just as if they were indubitable, as has been said above [Part Three, maxim two]; but since then I desired to attend only to the search for truth, I thought it necessary that I do ex-

actly the opposite, and that I reject as false
everything in which I could imagine the least
doubt, so as to see whether, after this pro-
cess, anything in my set of beliefs remains
that is entirely indubitable.

DESCARTES: I trust you understand, Socrates, that
there is no real contradiction between this choice
to doubt all things and the second maxim of my provisional code of morals in Part Three, even though
the two are exact opposites. For the theoretical enterprise, the search for truth, is not the same as the
practical enterprise, which concerns action.

SOCRATES: I understand. It's all in Aristotle, after all.

DESCARTES: And I trust you also understand, Socrates, that my rejecting as false every idea that I find
at all doubtable is not skepticism but the road to its
refutation. It is indeed a *universal* doubt, but it is only
a *methodological* doubt. And this means two things:
that it is not a lived, practiced doubt (I made that
clear by my distinction between theory and practice)
and that even within the theoretical realm, it is only
a method, to be used at the start, not a conclusion,
not my final and settled conviction, as it is for the
skeptics.

SOCRATES: That too is clear, from your last words.
So let us then examine this doubt in detail.

DESCARTES: I mention three parts of it here, and I
will add a fourth part from my *Meditations*, in order
to be more complete. (The *Meditations* does not appear in my hand, like the *Discourse on Method*, since
our task is only to explore this shorter book, but I re-

member what I wrote in the *Meditations* well enough
to supply it here when we come to the fourth part.)

[1] **Thus, since our senses sometimes deceive us, I decided to suppose that nothing was exactly as our senses would have us
imagine.**

DM 4,
para. 1

You see, Socrates, our senses *sometimes* seem to deceive us, and when we are being deceived, we do
not know that we are being deceived—otherwise, it
would not be deception. So we cannot *know* that the
things we perceive at this moment are really as they
seem.

[2] **And since there are men who err in reasoning, even in the simplest matters in geometry, and commit paralogisms, judging that
I was just as prone to err as the next man, I
rejected as false all the reasonings that I had
previously taken for demonstrations.**

DM 4,
para. 1

Again, Socrates, our powers of reasoning, like our
senses, are not infallible and sometimes deceive us.
And when we are deceived by our own errors, we do
not know that we are deceived, but believe we have
found the truth. So we cannot know that the things
we seem to have proved by reasoning at the present
time are not in that situation.

[3] **And finally, taking into account the fact
that the same thoughts we have when we
are awake can also come to us when we are
asleep, without any of the latter thoughts being true, I resolved to pretend that every-**

DM 4,
para. 1

thing that had ever entered my mind was no more true than the illusions of my dreams.

Once again, Socrates, we remember being deceived about all things in the world, things sensory as well as things rational, by our dreams. Some dreams seem so utterly real to us that when we wake up we are amazed to find that they are not real, as they seemed, but only dreams. How do we know that we are not in just such a dream now, one that seems so utterly real that we do not doubt it while we are in it?

And here is the fourth part of my doubt, from the *Meditations*:

[4] **Thus I will suppose not a supremely good God, the source of truth, but rather an evil genius, as clever and deceitful as he is powerful, who has directed his entire effort to misleading me. I will regard the heavens, the air, the earth, colors, shapes, sounds, and all external things as nothing but the deceptive games of my dreams, with which he lays snares for my credulity. I will regard myself as having no hands, no eyes, no flesh, no blood, no senses, but as nevertheless falsely believing that I possess all these things. I will remain resolutely fixed in this meditation, and, even if it be out of my power to know anything true, certainly it is within my power to take care resolutely to withhold my assent to what is false, lest this deceiver, powerful and clever as he is, have an effect on me.**

M I,
para. 12

For if there were such a being, he would be able to deceive me far more effectively and continuously than my senses, my reasonings, or my dreams.

SOCRATES: These four steps are certainly an interesting thought-experiment for a student, especially a young person who is at the age when doubts first arise naturally to his mind. I think he will be fascinated by a teacher who raises even further doubts in his mind, and this student will probably try to answer these doubts, and he will probably fail. And then he may for a moment actually wonder whether it is in fact true that he is in a dream, or being hypnotized by an evil spirit—he may even entertain for a moment the feeling of paranoia that would threaten him if he actually believed and lived this doubt—and this will be an exciting challenge to the student, which will take him far beyond your merely methodological "thought-experiment", even though I think that was not your intention. You do not suggest that he seriously believe the doubt, but only entertain it in the mind for a moment, as a "thought-experiment"; but an excitable young person will probably use your "thought-experiment" in a much more personal way —a way later philosophers will call "existential".

DESCARTES: I am not responsible for the misuses of my clearly stated intentions by excitable youth!

SOCRATES: I am not saying that you are responsible for that, or for the serious and deliberate "existentialist" philosophers who will reinterpret your doubt as existential rather than theoretical. I understand that for you this is merely a methodological thought-experiment.

DESCARTES: But that does not make it dispensable. It is not only a very useful thought-experiment, it is also a necessary one, for it alone makes my doubt truly universal. All other philosophers began with something; I am the first to begin with nothing.

SOCRATES: But you are beginning with something.

DESCARTES: Indeed I am not! Why do you say that?

SOCRATES: Because you are doing something.

DESCARTES: What am I doing?

SOCRATES: Exactly what you say you are doing: you are beginning with nothing.

DESCARTES: Oh. Then you agree. I pass the test of the touchstone.

SOCRATES: Let us not be too hasty. Beginning with nothing—is this not something?

DESCARTES: It is an act, a choice, a decision, of course. But it is not a premise.

SOCRATES: I understand. But I want to investigate that act for just a moment, if you please. Would you describe it as the act of choosing to doubt everything?

DESCARTES: Exactly.

SOCRATES: And doubting—would you call that the act of thrusting aside all the opinions you find in your mind?

DESCARTES: Yes.

SOCRATES: Is this not to assume that you have these opinions?

DESCARTES: Well, of course. But I do not assume that they are true. We must distinguish two ideas: that an opinion exists in my mind, and that that opinion is true.

SOCRATES: Good. Let us then distinguish these two ideas—that an opinion truly exists in your mind, in what we may call subjective reality, and that the opinion is true, true about objective reality. Now, it seems that you *are* assuming the first of these two ideas— that your ideas exist, and therefore that your mind exists, and therefore that you exist—even though you do *not* assume the *second* of these two ideas, namely, that any of these ideas in your mind is true. You do not assume the truth of any ideas—except these three: the idea that you have ideas, and therefore that you have a mind, and therefore that you exist.

DESCARTES: I later prove all of these things, Socrates. First I will prove that I exist, by my famous "I think, therefore I am." I will prove that of all the ideas in my mind, this is the one that cannot possibly be false. Then I will prove that my very essence is to be a mind, a thinker. And then I will explore the ideas in this thinker's mind, without assuming anything else, and I will find that there is one other idea in my mind that cannot possibly be false, which proves itself, so to speak, just as the "I think, therefore I am" proves itself, and that is the idea of God. I will give perfectly logical arguments for all these things. Shall we examine these arguments now?

SOCRATES: As I said before, let us not be so hasty. You say you later *prove* your existence and your essence as a thinker. But here, at the very beginning, in the act of doubting all your ideas, you seem to be *assuming* those two very same things, namely, your existence and your essence. For this act of doubting is an act of thinking, and this act really exists, and a real act comes from a real actor. So you seem to be assuming, at the beginning, two of the things you claim to be proving later.

Now you have studied logic, I'm sure. Please tell me what logicians call this procedure of assuming the very things you later claim to prove.

DESCARTES: Logicians call that the fallacy of "begging the question". But I do not commit that fallacy here, Socrates. I do not *assume* either my existence or my essence; I simply *use* them to doubt all things, and then, exploring this act of doubting, I logically deduce my existence and my nature as doubter and thinker. I begin by doubting, which is a form of thinking, and I deduce that in order to think I must exist, so I have proved my own existence. *Cogito ergo sum.* What do you think could be wrong with that procedure? Surely that is not begging the question. If it is, then every argument begs the question.

SOCRATES: Perhaps you do not beg the question, then. But . . .

DESCARTES: You always have a "but", don't you?

SOCRATES: Yes. That is my nature. I think I doubt both more and less than you do: more, because I have this question about your doubt that you do not;

and less, because I begin with methodic faith rather than methodic doubt.

DESCARTES: What is your doubt about my doubt?

SOCRATES: Let me try to explain. Your act of doubting everything—this is a choice, is it not? A choice that philosophers before you did not make, and which you did?

DESCARTES: That is correct.

SOCRATES: So let us explore what it means to make a choice. Would you say that flailing out blindly with your arms in the dark, as you sleep, is a choice?

DESCARTES: No.

SOCRATES: What about being born? Did you choose to be born?

DESCARTES: No.

SOCRATES: What about writing this book of yours? Was that a choice?

DESCARTES: Yes.

SOCRATES: And answering my questions rather than remaining silent, and answering them in the way that you do—is that a choice?

DESCARTES: Yes.

SOCRATES: Do you see, then, what must be present for there to be a choice?

DESCARTES: I think so. Intelligence must be present.

SOCRATES: When you are dreaming, and flailing blindly, is the dreamer a creature with intelligence?

DESCARTES: Yes. He is a human being.

SOCRATES: But is that act an act guided by intelligence?

DESCARTES: No. It is an animal act.

SOCRATES: Then intelligence must be not only present but operating, guiding the act, if we are to call the act a choice.

DESCARTES: That is correct.

SOCRATES: And intelligence cannot operate except on some object.

DESCARTES: True again.

SOCRATES: And when the intelligence operates on an object, we say that object is known, or intelligized, or understood, do we not?

DESCARTES: Yes.

SOCRATES: So choice presupposes knowledge.

DESCARTES: Yes.

SOCRATES: And you have made a choice to doubt all things.

DESCARTES: Yes.

SOCRATES: Therefore that choice presupposes some knowledge.

DESCARTES: Yes: the knowledge that I have certain ideas in my mind, but not whether any of these ideas are true or not.

SOCRATES: But you said you were doubting *all* knowledge. Yet we have found an act of knowledge presupposed in the act of doubting.

DESCARTES: I would not call that an act of knowledge, nor would I say that I am presupposing it.

SOCRATES: But if you did not doubt, your mind would continue to act as it usually acts, accepting certain ideas as true without proof and going on from there, as we all do every day. Is this not so?

DESCARTES: Yes.

SOCRATES: And you must first put a stop to this ordinary way of thinking, if you are to doubt all things. Is this not so?

DESCARTES: Yes.

SOCRATES: And this act of putting a stop to ordinary thinking—this is a choice, is it not?

DESCARTES: Yes.

SOCRATES: And we admitted that every choice presupposes some knowledge, did we not?

DESCARTES: We did.

SOCRATES: So it looks as if you must presuppose some knowledge in order to doubt all things.

DESCARTES: In that sense, yes.

SOCRATES: But doubting all things is the choice *not* to presuppose anything.

DESCARTES: That is what it is.

SOCRATES: So you must presuppose something in order *not* to presuppose anything. So it seems as if your starting point is logically self-contradictory.

DESCARTES: The Scholastics had a motto: "To avoid a contradiction, make a distinction." I think I can find a distinction somewhere in your argument that would save me, if we only reviewed each step of the argument more carefully. As you say, let us not be too hasty.

SOCRATES: Let me grant you that. Let us pretend that you have already made such a saving distinction and passed this test. We have endless time here to come back to this point if we wish, and our readers have plenty of time to review it too. They might want to add other questions to mine, such as: Is it possible to doubt the laws of logic in a meaningful way? Do you not use them, and thus presuppose them? But for now, let us return to your actual text, for we have been away from it for too long, like boats out of sight of land.

14

Step Two of Descartes' Philosophical System: "I Think, Therefore I Am"

SOCRATES: Here is the single most famous point of your philosophy, perhaps the single most famous sentence in the whole history of philosophy, and the foundation for everything else in it. For without the *cogito ergo sum*, you could go no further. Is that not correct?

DESCARTES: Yes. And the advantage of my foundation over all others is that it is simple. It is just this one point, not a whole host of questionable assumptions, such as you and Plato and Aristotle began with.

SOCRATES: So your philosophical system is like an upside-down pyramid, resting on this single point.

DESCARTES: An arresting image. But surely you are not going to argue from this image and say that no building can rest on a single point, and therefore no philosophy can either. A pyramid stands because its point is at the top; it would not stand if its point were at the bottom. But building a philosophy is not like building a pyramid. Philosophy, like geometry, proves many things from a few things, or even from one thing.

SOCRATES: No, that is not the point of my analogy.

DESCARTES: What is the point, then?

SOCRATES: That if this point collapses, your entire system collapses.

DESCARTES: That is true. I accept that parallel. In fact, I make it, in the *Meditations*, with my analogy of the fulcrum, the "Archimedean point":

M 2,
para. 1

> **Archimedes sought only a firm and immovable point in order to move the entire earth from one place to another. Surely great things are to be hoped for if I am lucky enough to find at least one thing that is certain and indubitable.**

As said earlier, when Archimedes discovered the lever, and its power, he supposedly said, "Give me only a lever long enough and a fulcrum to rest it on, and I can move the entire world." And that is my claim: to have found the immovable, indubitable point on which the lever of all philosophical arguments can rest, and to move the whole world of thought thereby.

SOCRATES: Then our investigation of this point is utterly crucial—for your entire philosophy, and for the whole history of modern philosophy insofar as it stems from yours.

DESCARTES: I accept this great responsibility, Socrates. Examine away; I am certain that my foundation will stand.

SOCRATES: To examine it, we must first have it before us. Here are your words, from the *Discourse on Method*, and then your longer version, from the *Medications*.

DESCARTES: You mean *Meditations*.

SOCRATES: Oh, yes. Sorry. That was what they will later call a "Freudian slip". Here is the passage:

> **But immediately after** [these doubts] **I noticed that, during the time I wanted thus to think everything was false, it was necessary that I, who thought thus, be something. And noticing that this truth—*I think, therefore I am*—was so firm and so certain that the most extravagant suppositions of the skeptics were unable to shake it, I judged that I could accept it without scruple as the first principle of the philosophy I was seeking.**

DM 4, para. 1

And here is the longer passage, from the *Meditations*:

> **I have persuaded myself that there is nothing at all in the world: no heaven, no earth, no minds, no bodies. Is it not then true that I do not exist? But certainly I should exist, if I were to persuade myself of something. But there is a deceiver (I know not who he is) powerful and sly in the highest degree, who is always purposely deceiving me. Then there is no doubt that I exist, if he deceives me. And deceive me as he will, he can never bring it about that I am nothing so long**

M 2, para. 3

as I shall think that I am something. Thus it must be granted that, after weighing everything carefully and sufficiently, one must come to the considered judgment that the statement "I am, I exist" is necessarily true every time it is uttered by me or conceived in my mind.

Which of these two versions do you want to defend?

DESCARTES: The second one.

SOCRATES: And why is that?

DESCARTES: Because in the first version I tried to *prove* that I exist by an argument, a syllogism: "*Cogito ergo sum*," "I think, therefore I am." In the second version, which I published four years later, I claimed that the *proposition* ("*statement*") "I am, I exist" is necessarily true.

SOCRATES: Why did you change the first version? Did you find a fallacy in your argument?

DESCARTES: Not a formal fallacy. My syllogism was logically valid. It was an enthymeme, a syllogism with an implied premise: that whatever thinks, exists. Thus, whatever thinks, exists; I think; therefore I exist. But the French version of this argument showed me something that the Latin did not. In French, as in English, the pronoun and the verb are two distinct words, but in Latin they are one. When we say, "Je pense, donc je suis", or, "I think, therefore I am", we see what seems to be a material fallacy. Do you see it, Socrates?

SOCRATES: I think I do. I believe it is "begging the question", assuming in the premise what you are supposed to be proving in the conclusion.

DESCARTES: Yes, that is what I perceived too. I tried to *prove* the "I", but instead I *assumed* that there was an "I" behind the "think".

SOCRATES: And the next great philosopher to use your mathematical method, Baruch Spinoza, denied that assumption. He not only noted that you had not *proved* the existence of an "I" but he actually *denied* the existence of the "I", the individual self, as a "substance" or entity separate from other substances. He was a pantheist and said that only one substance existed, which he called both God and Nature. So his version of your starting point would be simply that "thinking exists". But in no way can "I exist" be proved simply from the premise that "thinking exists", unless all thinking is thinking by an "I", which is what he denied.

DESCARTES: That is why I changed the wording of this all-important starting point when I wrote the *Meditations*. If I were to reword it in Latin, I would say not *cogito* ergo *sum* but *cogito* sive *sum*—I think, or I exist. I think, in other words I exist. I think, that is to say, I exist. It is a single proposition, not a syllogism.

SOCRATES: I see another reason why you cannot begin with a syllogism, either this one or any other.

DESCARTES: I think I know what you are going to say, Socrates. May I guess?

SOCRATES: Be my guess—guest.

DESCARTES: I am trying to refute skepticism with my new system of philosophy. And one of the oldest arguments of the skeptic is this one: if we begin by questioning everything, as I do, we cannot simply accept any idea without proof. We cannot be certain of any conclusion until we have given a proof of it. But a proof is a demonstration of the truth of a conclusion by deducing it from premises. But we must then question those premises and demand proof for *them*. And those proofs, in turn, need premises, which need to be questioned and proved, et cetera, et cetera, ad infinitum. So *no* syllogism can be the first, absolute certainty.

SOCRATES: That is exactly what I was thinking. You are a very clear and logical thinker, René.

DESCARTES: Why thank you, Socrates. I have always thought of us as kindred spirits.

SOCRATES: I did not say that. I merely said that you were a very clear and logical thinker. And if you confuse being a very clear and logical thinker with being a kindred spirit, that shows that you are *not* a very clear and logical thinker.

DESCARTES: Oh. But the substantive point is that my revised starting point is sound, because it is a self-evident proposition.

SOCRATES: Perhaps we should be sure we both understand what "a self-evident proposition" means.

DESCARTES: Indeed. Well, then, let me put it into the very basic context of elementary logic, with its "three acts of the mind". All thought is composed first of all of concepts, which are expressed in words or phrases, which logicians call terms; and then these are the subjects and predicates of propositions, declarative sentences; and then these propositions are the premises and conclusions of arguments. Terms are either clear or unclear, but in themselves neither true nor false. Propositions are either true or false, and arguments are either logically valid or logically invalid, depending on whether the conclusion follows with logical necessity from the premises.

Now there are two kinds of propositions: true and false. And among true propositions, there are also two kinds: some are self-evident and some are not. My starting point is a self-evident proposition.

SOCRATES: What makes a proposition self-evident?

DESCARTES: There are three answers to that question. The first one is psychological and the other two are logical, that is, matters of formal logic.

First, a self-evident proposition is one that we can know with certainty to be true without any proof, without any premises.

Second, the reason we can know that is because the predicate does not add anything new to the subject. Examples of this would be "Two plus two equals four" and "a whole is greater than any one of its parts" and "whatever has attributes A, B, and C, has attribute B", and "X does not equal non-X". But "two plus Y equals four" is not self-evident, because Y might not be 2, and in that case the proposition would be false. "Goliath is bigger than David" is true, but not self-evident, like "the whole is greater than the part". Goliath might shrink to a dwarf without ceasing to be Goliath, and David might grow to be a giant without ceasing to be David, and then the proposition "Goliath is bigger than David" would be false. "Whatever is human, and French, and female, has a womb" is true, but not self-evident, since one could surgically remove the womb from one French woman and then the proposition would be false.

The third definition of a self-evident proposition is one whose contradictory is self-contradictory. If you deny it, you contradict yourself. You need no other propositions, as premises, to know that $2 + 2 = 4$ or that whatever has A, B, and C has B, because if you say that $2 + 2$ are not 4, or that something that has A, B, and C does not have B, you have contradicted yourself.

SOCRATES: I think that was an admirably clear answer, René, and a logically impeccable one.

DESCARTES: So do you now intend to peck at the impeccable, as is your wont?

SOCRATES: No, I accept your three definitions. All we need to do is to use them to see whether your starting point of *cogito sive sum* is self-evident or not.

DESCARTES: Clearly, it is, Socrates. All men are certain of their existence as soon as they utter the proposition "I exist." No one seeks proof of it, no one doubts it, no one argues about it.

SOCRATES: So it passes the first test, the psychological test.

DESCARTES: Yes, and it also passes the third test, for if I say, "I do not exist", I clearly contradict myself. So much so that I become an instant laughingstock. And since the third test is simply the negative version of the second one, I pass the second test too.

SOCRATES: Let us not be too hasty. For the whole of your philosophy depends on this one point, remember, your "Archimedean point". Let us be very careful not to miss anything here.

DESCARTES: What could we miss? The point is as simple as 2 + 2 = 4.

SOCRATES: Well, we have not yet applied your second definition of a self-evident proposition to your new starting point.

DESCARTES: Then let us do that. I'm sure we will find that "I am" is indeed a self-evident proposition.

SOCRATES: Every proposition has a subject term and a predicate term, correct?

DESCARTES: Yes.

SOCRATES: And what is the subject of "I am"?

DESCARTES: "I".

SOCRATES: And the predicate?

DESCARTES: "Am".

SOCRATES: And what is the relation between the predicate and the subject in a self-evident proposition?

DESCARTES: The predicate does not add any accident to the subject, like "I am hot", or "Green trees are pleasant", but merely restates the essence of the subject, like "I am I", or "Green trees are trees."

SOCRATES: And the predicate here is "am", or existence.

DESCARTES: Yes.

SOCRATES: And the subject is "I"?

DESCARTES: Yes.

SOCRATES: And this "I" is not Socrates, or Gabriel, or God, but René Descartes?

DESCARTES: Of course.

SOCRATES: It seems to me, then, that you and Spinoza quite agree about pantheism.

DESCARTES: What do you mean by that?

SOCRATES: That you seem to be confusing yourself with God. Other than that minor confusion, though, I think your system passes muster . . .

DESCARTES: Wait! What do you mean, that I confuse myself with God? What a ridiculous charge!

SOCRATES: Well, in saying that "I exist" is a self-evident proposition, do you not say that its predicate is essential to its subject?

DESCARTES: Yes. That is what a self-evident proposition means.

SOCRATES: And does this not mean that you are saying that your existence, which is your predicate, is essential to your "I", which is your subject?

DESCARTES: Yes, for "existence" is my predicate and "I" is my subject.

SOCRATES: So you are saying that your existence is your essence.

DESCARTES: Oh.

SOCRATES: I thought that in your theology that was true only of God. That is why God needs no creator to give Him existence, while everything else does: His very essence is to exist, but creatures need an external cause to exist.

DESCARTES: Oops.

SOCRATES: An eloquent short act of contrition!

DESCARTES: It is true that my existence is contingent, not necessary. I did not have to exist. In fact, before I was conceived, I did not exist. So my existence is *not* self-evident in this sense—only God's is. So "I am" is a self-evident proposition only for God, not for any creature.

SOCRATES: You see, now, why I said that when you begin with "I am", and declare this self-evident, you confuse your essence with God's, and your name with the name God revealed to Moses from the burning bush: "I AM".

So this is indeed a radical new beginning. Medieval man began with the divine "I AM", but you become the first truly modern man, since you begin with the human "I am".

DESCARTES: No, no, no. That would be heresy, and blasphemy, and nothing could be farther from my intention.

And yet my "I am" meets the other two criteria for a self-evident proposition. How can equally valid criteria for the same thing yield opposite results?

SOCRATES: I don't think they do. If you examine the third criterion more carefully, you will see that the proposition that you do not exist is not self-contradictory at all. In fact, it was *true* that you did not exist for many centuries before you came to be.

DESCARTES: So the two logical criteria yield the same result. But the first one, the psychological one, yields the opposite result. Now why is that? Why is "I am" psychologically self-evident if it is not logically self-evident?

SOCRATES: You yourself seem to have realized this when you added these crucial words to your later version, in the *Meditations*: **"that the statement 'I am, I exist' is necessarily true** *every time it is uttered by me or conceived in my mind*." It is necessarily true, or self-evident, that you exist *only to you*, only subjectively, only psychologically; but the proposition is not self-evident in itself, nor to anyone else. It is not objectively and logically self-evident.

DESCARTES: But I still have a starting point for my philosophy that is absolutely certain psychologically, or subjectively. Each human person can replicate this thought experiment himself. *My* existence will not be self-evident to him, but his *own* will be.

SOCRATES: That is true, but is that what you want and need to begin your system? You intended to begin a new kind of philosophy: Did you intend it to be more subjective than any previous philosophy, or more objective and logical and mathematical and scientific than any previous philosophy?

DESCARTES: I seem to have created a monster.

SOCRATES: I would not call it a monster. I would just call it . . . Existentialism.

15

Step Three of Descartes' Philosophical System: *"What* I Am" (Descartes' Anthropology)

SOCRATES: Your next point, after proving your first certainty, that you are, is to inquire *what* you are. And here is how you summarize this step in the next paragraph. . . .

DESCARTES: I am glad you understand that this is simply a summary, each paragraph of this fourth Part of my *Discourse on Method* summarizing a whole chapter of my longer *Meditations*, just as St. Thomas Aquinas summarized five long arguments for God's existence in five short paragraphs in his *Summa Theologiae*, but he took twenty times more space to state just the first of the five arguments in the *Summa Contra Gentiles*.

SOCRATES: Yes, but, human nature being what it is, it is usually the shorter version, and the shorter book, that becomes more popular and influential. In any case, that is the book we are examining now. So here is your short version of your anthropology, your answer to the question of "know thyself", the question I made famous:

Then, examining with attention what I was, and seeing that I could pretend [conceive] that I had no body and that there was no world nor any place where I was, but that I could not pretend, on that account, that I did not exist; and that, on the contrary, from the very fact that I thought about doubting the truth of other things, it followed very evidently and very certainly that I existed. On the other hand, had I simply stopped thinking, even if all the rest of what I have ever imagined were true, I would have no reason to believe that I existed. From this I knew that I was a substance the whole essence or nature of which was merely to think, and which, in order to exist, needed no place and depended on no material thing. Thus this "I," that is, the soul through which I am what I am, is entirely distinct from the body, and is even easier to know than the body, and even if there were no body, the soul would not cease to be all that it is.

DM 4, para. 2

Your premises seem to be true. At any rate, most people would agree with them. But your conclusion seems, to most people, untrue. At any rate, most people would disagree with it. They believe their bodies and their souls *together* make up their essence. So we must explore your logic: Do your premises prove your conclusion? That is a fair question, is it not?

DESCARTES: Indeed it is. If there is anything I claim to be, it is to be logical. If my argument is not logical, it is worthless.

SOCRATES: Let us first examine your premise. I suspect that many people, especially those of a common-
sense bent, will claim that it is impossible and un-
thinkable; that you cannot really think, or pretend,
or conceive, or believe, that you have no body, and
that no bodies or spaces exist at all. How would you
answer these people?

DESCARTES: By pointing out that there are many,
many people who not only pretend that this is so
as a thought-experiment, as I suggest here, but who
actually believe that it is literally true. For there are
some forms of Hindu and Buddhist philosophy that
teach that nothing in fact exists except Mind, whether
this Mind is divine or human; and that all that we usually believe exists outside Mind—our own bodies, and
other people's bodies, and the bodies in the world,
and the universe itself, and all space and time in the
universe as well as all the matter in it—that all these
things are really only thoughts.

Many Hindus believe that these things are the
dreams of Brahman, which occur during a *kalpa* cycle,
or a "night of Brahman", and which disappear when
Brahman awakens and a "day of Brahman" begins.
They say that these things, being only dreams, are
"maya", or illusions.

Many Buddhists believe that they are illusions too,
but illusions of *human* thought when it is deluded,
or sleeping, or unenlightened. (For Buddhists do not
speak of a God.) In both versions, the Hindu and the
Buddhist, all these illusions disappear upon waking,
either the waking of Brahman or the waking of our-

selves. So my premise is indeed thinkable. We *can* think away bodies, including our own bodies.

But we cannot think away our minds. That is what I just proved with my *cogito ergo sum*. Even if all our thoughts of matter are delusions, or dreams, or deceptions produced by the devil hypnotizing us, there is one thought that cannot be false, the thought that I am thinking. For in order to be deceived, I must think. It is as necessary a demonstration as the previous one, that in order to think, I must exist.

SOCRATES: Your premise seems secure. But you seem to leap from this premise to a conclusion that most people would say does not logically follow from that premise and is also in fact false. That is what most people would say. The conclusion is: **"From this I knew that I was a substance the whole essence or nature of which was merely to think, and which, in order to exist, needed no place and depended on no material thing."** And then you derive three more closely related conclusions, or corollaries. You say **"Thus, this 'I,' that is, the soul through which I am what I am, is entirely distinct from the body, and is even easier to know than the body, and even if there were no body, the soul would not cease to be all that it is."**
So your conclusion is

DM 4, para. 2

  1. that your whole essence is thought,
  2. that you do not need a body or matter to exist,
  3. that your soul is entirely distinct from your body,
  4. that it is easier to know than the body, and

5. that no part of your soul's nature is dependent on the body, for "even if there were no body, the soul would not cease to be all that it is."

Most people would believe, instead, that all five of these propositions are false. Let us call their belief "Aristotelianism", just to have a single name for it. So here is how I would set out the five differences between your anthropology and Aristotle's (which was also adopted by St. Thomas Aquinas, with the addition of immortality, which Aristotle omitted). Aristotelians believe the opposite of each of your five propositions. They believe that

1. First of all, your whole essence is not merely to be a spiritual soul but to be a soul-body compound; that your essence, and the essence of any human being, includes an animal body as well as a spiritual soul, for that is how we differ from angels, just as we differ from animals by possessing a spiritual soul.

2. Second, they believe that that for this essence to exist, the material body that is part of that essence must also exist. That logically follows from the first point.

3. Third, they believe that the soul, though it is *different* from the body, is not *distinct* from it. In other words, though the soul is not just one more kind of body, like another chemical element, yet it is not a distinct, independent substance, or being, or entity. And even most of those people who agree with you that the mind *is* a distinct substance from the body would say at least that it is *dependent* on the body for its activity, as a swordsman is dependent on his sword. And the Aristotelians would go further and

say it is not even a distinct substance from the body but rather the "form" or life of the body, related to it somewhat as the meaning of a book is related to the words of the book.

4. Fourth, they believe that the body is easier to know than the soul, since all learning begins with bodily sense experience, and we can sense bodies but not souls with the five senses.

5. And fifth, they believe that if there were no body, the soul would not be what it is, since what it is, is "the form, or life, of the body". Thus this point follows logically from the third point.

DESCARTES: Well stated, Socrates. All five of these conclusions are bound up together and can be deduced from each other.

SOCRATES: At least number 2 follows from number 1, and number 5 from number 3. And number 4, the point about which is easier to know, also follows from number 1, since if the soul is your whole essence, if you are only a soul, that is the *only* thing knowable about your essence; but if your essence also includes a body, then *that* is easier to know, since it is easier to use our senses than our reason. Infants, like animals, have senses that work well and know much, but only later do infants learn to use their reason.

So we are left with only two differences rather than five, since the other three logically follow from these two. Is your whole essence thought, and are your body and your soul two distinct substances?

DESCARTES: I accept your analysis. You are a paragon of logic, Socrates. But I would go one step further: I think the second of these two points logically follows from the first one. For if my whole essence is thought, then see what follows: since only the soul can think, by its power of mind, while the body cannot think (though it can be used as the soul's instrument while it is alive, as a sword by a swordsman or a calculating machine by a mathematician), it follows that soul and body must be distinct substances.

SOCRATES: Why does that logically follow?

DESCARTES: You can clearly see this by looking at analogies, or similar cases. If only fire can burn, while water cannot, they must be distinct substances. If only God can create, while creatures cannot, they must be distinct substances. If only plants can grow, while rocks cannot, they must be distinct substances.

So if I prove my first point, that our whole essence is thought, I have proved the whole of my anthropology. For all the other points follow.

SOCRATES: That seems to be the case. So what is your proof that our whole essence is thought?

DESCARTES: I stated it in the first half of my paragraph. I can think away my body but I cannot think away my mind. I cannot without self-contradiction doubt my thinking, but I can without self-contradiction doubt my body, as we saw in the case of the Hindu and the Buddhist.

SOCRATES: And from this you argue that it logically follows that your whole essence is mind, not body?

DESCARTES: Yes.

SOCRATES: Do you see the hidden premise of this argument?

DESCARTES: Yes. What I cannot without self-contradiction doubt is the essence, and what I can without self-contradiction doubt is not the essence.

SOCRATES: This seems to be a self-evident premise. And with this premise, you seem to have proved your conclusion. And your conclusion is that your whole essence is mind.

But this conclusion is shockingly contradictory to Aristotelian common sense. And one of the corollaries of your conclusion, that your mind and your body are two distinct substances, is even more shockingly contradictory to Aristotelian common sense, and to every school of anthropology, psychology, and psychiatry that will ever exist. Neither common sense nor the sciences of man accept your two-substance theory; they all side with Aristotle. Aristotelian philosophers call it "hylomorphism", or matter-and-form-ism. Psychologists call it the "psychosomatic unity". Common sense simply calls it "me", using the very same word for both mind and body: "my" mind and "my" body.

So this is a crucial point in your philosophy, the point at which you come into the most violent contradiction to the rest of the world.

And if you are right, you have given to philosophy what seems like an unanswerable question: If the mind and the body are two distinct substances, how can they interact so perfectly that they seem to be one thing? Our daily and hourly experience seems to confirm Aristotle's anthropology and disprove yours.

Our mind and body seem to act together like the words and the meaning of a book, rather than like the swordsman and the sword, or the captain and the ship, or the master and the slave, or the rider and the horse, or the mathematician and his calculating machine. If you are right, how do you explain the appearances, the experiences that seem to disprove your theory?

This "mind-body problem" will bedevil your successors and produce extravagant and unbelievable solutions, such as Malebranche's "occasionalism", which supposes that there are two separate worlds, minds and bodies, spirit and matter, and that God causes all events in both worlds on the occasion of His perceiving a corresponding event in the other world; that if I were to slap you in the face, it would not be my hand's action that causes your surprise and pain but God's action on your soul. Another of your successors, with the strange name of Geulincx, supposed that God set up a "pre-established harmony" between the two totally distinct worlds of mind and matter at creation, like two alarm clocks set to tell the same time.

Worse than these intellectual puzzles, your dualism between mind and matter will also bedevil the very life of Western civilization, for your two categories of mindless matter and matterless mind, or thinking substance and spatially extended substance, will come to seem so clear and distinct to the people of this civilization that they will not only *think* in terms of your mind-body dualism but also *live* that way, experiencing an alienation between mind and body, spirit and matter, man and nature, which no previous culture in history ever did. And you will be largely blamed for this.

DESCARTES: I care not about blame; I care about error. Will I be refuted?

SOCRATES: Alas, you will usually be blamed instead of being refuted.

DESCARTES: I should not be blamed unless I am refuted.

SOCRATES: I agree.

DESCARTES: So refute me, and I will begin again.

SOCRATES: That is precisely the purpose of this place.

DESCARTES: I wait with bated breath.

SOCRATES: You may have to wait a little longer. For the adequate refutation of your mind-body dualism will have to be rather difficult and technical, and perhaps this is not the place or time for it. Instead, let me offer a simpler and easier refutation. Logicians call it a *reductio ad absurdum* proof. Instead of directly disproving a theory, if we can show that it logically leads to consequences that are so absurd that they can be known with certainty to be false, then it logically follows that the theory is false, even though we may not know *why* it is false, or how to disprove it in any other way.

It is a perfectly valid logical argument to say that if A, then B, but B is false, therefore A must be false. And if B is not only false but so obviously false that it is absurd, then we have the "reduction to absurdity" proof against A.

Now most people would argue that that is adequate refutation of your anthropology. For they would say that it is much more certain that your conclusion is false than that your premise is true.

DESCARTES: Why?

SOCRATES: Because your conclusion is that each human being is two substances, spirit and matter, a ghost in a machine. And that is so absurd that only those with serious psychological disorders believe it.

DESCARTES: Most people may indeed believe what you say—I do not know, I did not take a poll of all individuals and cultures in history. But we do not find truth by "counting noses". And even if every single person believed my conclusion was absurd, that is not an adequate refutation of it for me, Socrates. I want to know where I went wrong, if I did. Merely to know that it is wrong is not satisfactory. And merely to know that many people, or most people, or even all people, believe that it is wrong does not prove that it is wrong. I will not accept the idea that my conclusion, or my corollary, is absurd just because most people think so. That is the kind of thinking that held science back for two thousand years: *"Everyone* agrees with the great Aristotle, so let us not question him."

SOCRATES: I agree, René: we must use logical proofs, and not just opinion polls. So someone—myself, perhaps—must stand up for this popular opinion and translate it into a logical reason. Someone must find the error in your apparently perfectly logical argument.

But I would prefer not to search for that right now. Once again, for the sake of anyone who may be reading this conversation, I would like to leave this large hole in our argument so that the reader can pursue it and try to fill it himself, rather than simply watching us fill in all the holes in our argument. For I think that this hole-filling enterprise will be so abstract and technical that most readers will be deterred from it, though erstwhile logicians will take to it like an otter to a mudslide.

DESCARTES: You are the master of the procedure here, Socrates, so if that is what you say we should do, then that is what we shall do. I accept your authority in this place, for I am the examinee, not the examiner. But could you satisfy my curiosity by answering me one question about my legacy to the philosophers who came after me regarding this problem of human nature?

SOCRATES: I might. What is your question?

DESCARTES: Did anyone solve the problem of how the mind is related to the body? I know I did not give an adequate answer to that question. I thought that perhaps the answer would come from the physiologists, who in my time had discovered the first ductless gland, the pineal gland, at the base of the brain. I thought that since this free-floating gland was not physically attached to the rest of the body in the way that all other body parts are, it might be the seat of the soul. But I think now that this was a rather foolish error. For a gland, whether ductless or not, is a purely material thing, and not a bridge between matter and mind at all. Ductlessness does not equal immateriality.

So did anyone find a better answer than I did to this mysterious question of how these two totally different things, the mind and the body, are so perfectly related that they seem to behave as one thing?

SOCRATES: No. But someone did find a better answer than you did to another question: the question of why no one ever found an adequate answer to that question. Are you interested?

DESCARTES: Very.

SOCRATES: His name was Gabriel Marcel, and he lived three hundred years after you. Like you he was French, and Catholic. And he distinguished all the questions philosophers ask into two categories: what he called "problems" and what he called "mysteries". By "mysteries" he meant not merely questions that were not yet clear or not yet answered, but questions that in principle could never become totally clear or adequately answered, as any "problem" could, for this reason: because in a "mystery" the questioner "participates in" the question. He is involved, not detached. In other words, the real question is the questioner himself, and the questioner thus cannot objectify the question but must live the question even in the act of asking it.

DESCARTES: Exactly as I lived my existence in the very act of denying it! I think I understand Marcel's point, for that is precisely the point of my most famous argument, my *cogito ergo sum*. I cannot deny my existence because in the very act of denying it I must exist.

SOCRATES: Then perhaps you can see how this principle could be extended to other problems like the unity of the mind and the body, even though the body has no thought and the mind has no extension in space.

DESCARTES: What other "mysteries" did this philosopher mention?

SOCRATES: Love, death, evil, and beauty, especially the beauty of music, none of which have ever received totally clear and totally adequate explanations.

DESCARTES: I shall have to contemplate this possibility some time, though it seems utterly alien to my method, spirit, and intentions.

SOCRATES: As I said before, perhaps the most fruitful philosophy you invented was not the one you intended to invent at all but rather one that is "utterly alien to your method, spirit, and intentions": the philosophy of Existentialism.

16

Step Four of Descartes' Philosophical System: The Criterion of Truth

SOCRATES: Here is your next paragraph, and your next point:

DM 4, para. 3

After this, I considered in a general way what is needed for a proposition to be true and certain; for since I had just found a proposition that I knew was true, I thought I ought also know in what this certitude consists. And having noticed that there is nothing in all of this—*I think, therefore I am*—that assures me that I am uttering the truth, except that I see very clearly that, in order to think, one must exist; I judged that I could take as a general rule that the things we conceive very clearly and very distinctly are all true, but that there only remains some difficulty in properly discerning which are the ones that we distinctly conceive.

DESCARTES: My next step after I have proved my own existence and essence is to ask what else I can know. Where can I go from here? I cannot use my senses, for I have not yet proved them reliable. I have not proved that there is a God, or that there is any other mind than mine. All I have is my mind and its ideas. How can I know which of those ideas are true?

If I found a criterion for truth, a universal standard that I could apply to all my ideas, then I could use that criterion to judge my ideas and to distinguish the certainly true ones from the ones that might be false. All the ideas that passed this strict test I could know were true, and those that did not pass this test, I would continue to doubt.

SOCRATES: You say "criterion of *truth*" but you really mean "criterion of *certainty*". Are you perhaps confusing these two things?

DESCARTES: No, for I admit that many ideas may be true without being certain. My thirst was for certainty, as I explained in my little intellectual autobiography.

SOCRATES: I wonder whether that thirst was wholly healthy. But this is yet another question which we must leave to the ambitious reader to pursue. Go on.

DESCARTES: I believed that all men innately knew and used such a criterion, and said so in the very first paragraph of my book, where I asserted that reason was innate and equal in all men, and defined reason as the ability to distinguish the true from the false. One needs a criterion of truth to do that. So if we can do that, we must have the criterion. And if we have it, it remains only for me to bring out into the light that which is already present.

SOCRATES: And how do you find this criterion?

DESCARTES: Fortunately, I have already used it successfully in finding this one certain idea of my own existence. How did I come to this certainty? Only because I clearly perceived with my mind that *cogito ergo sum* was a clear and distinct idea. So the criterion of truth is the clarity and distinctness of an idea. Clarity is the positive half, distinctness the negative. Clarity is the relation between the idea and the mind, distinctness the relation between the idea and other ideas. An idea is clear if it is undoubtable, and distinct if it is unconfusable, if it cannot be confused with other ideas.

Now it was only because I used this criterion that I could be certain of the *"cogito ergo sum"*. So I have found my criterion for truth.

SOCRATES: Your argument for the criterion, then, is an inductive argument, from a particular example to a general principle. It worked in one case, therefore it will work in all cases.

DESCARTES: Oh, no, Socrates. Inductive arguments are only probable. And inductive arguments become more probable as the number of cases increases. And I have only one case, so this would be the weakest of all inductive arguments. It would at best be a clue, not a proof. It is like arguing that this swan is white, therefore all swans are white.

SOCRATES: So you must have a deductive argument, then, for this criterion of truth. Deductive arguments alone are certain.

DESCARTES: And I do. After I prove the existence of God, I also prove that God is perfect and therefore not a deceiver. And I also prove that God is the author of my being. Now if false ideas impressed themselves upon my mind with such force of clarity that I could not doubt them, God would be a deceiver. If my natural and proper use of my mind results in inevitable error, then God, the author and designer of my being, would be responsible for my error. Since this cannot be true, I can be confident that I am not deceived as long as I use my innate, God-given mental gifts correctly.

(Thus elsewhere I explain all error as due to our fault, our will insisting on judging beyond the evidence. Our will is free, but our mind is not. For instance, our will is free to choose to believe that God is good or that God is not good, but our mind is not free to believe that good is not good, or that God is not God, for that is self-contradictory. Ideas often come to the mind without our choice, and the laws of logic are not a matter of our choice; but our judgments proceed from the mind only by our choice, and choice always involves the will. So all error comes from our will, judging beyond the evidence.)

My argument about God's trustability is indeed a deductive argument for my criterion of truth, not an inductive one. And thus it is a certain argument, not just a probable one.

SOCRATES: Indeed it is. Whether it is a good deductive argument or not remains to be seen.

DESCARTES: We will see that when we come to my arguments for the existence of God, in the next paragraph.

SOCRATES: But that is just the problem: the premise for your argument comes after its conclusion.

DESCARTES: What do you mean?

SOCRATES: Your conclusion is that clear and distinct ideas are true.

DESCARTES: Yes.

SOCRATES: And your premise is that God is reliable.

DESCARTES: Yes.

SOCRATES: But you have not yet proved God.

DESCARTES: Oh.

SOCRATES: And when you do prove Him, you use your criterion of truth as a premise.

DESCARTES: Why do you say that?

SOCRATES: Because your proof cannot be taken from anything observed in the world, such as design, from which you would reason to a Designer, or the chain of causes and effects, from which you would reason to a first, un-caused Cause, because you have not yet proved the existence of the material world yet. This is still under doubt.

DESCARTES: That is true.

SOCRATES: So the only starting point for your proof for God must be the idea of God.

DESCARTES: That is also true.

SOCRATES: And your argument is essentially this, is it not?—the idea of God is a clear and distinct idea, an indubitable idea, therefore it is true.

DESCARTES: That is a very inadequate version of my proof.

SOCRATES: Oh, I admit that. I was not giving the logic of the proof—we will look at that next—but the method, or the strategy. And the strategy is this: you use the clear and distinct idea of God to prove the existence of God.

DESCARTES: That is true.

SOCRATES: But you also use God's existence and veracity to prove that you can trust your clear and distinct ideas.

DESCARTES: Oh.

SOCRATES: I think you know what logicians call that.

DESCARTES: It is a circular argument, or arguing in a circle. But I have a third proof of my criterion of clarity and distinctness. It is also deductive, but it does not presuppose God.

SOCRATES: I'm waiting.

DESCARTES: If the criterion were not valid, I could not have attained certainty about the *"cogito"*. For that argument used the criterion, at least implicitly. But the certainty it gave me was valid, therefore the criterion was. I merely brought the criterion up from the implicit to the explicit.

SOCRATES: Bringing the implicit up into the light of the explicit—this sounds exactly like Aristotle's theory of abstraction, which you reject as not explicit enough, not mathematical enough. Perhaps you are more Aristotelian than you think.

DESCARTES: I grant you that the way I establish my criterion of truth is not as clear as the criterion itself: is it inductive, deductive, or implicit? But do you see anything wrong with the criterion itself? In order to do that, you would have to find some clear and distinct idea that was not true. That would be the only way to refute my criterion of truth. For I do not claim that that all truth is clear and distinct —obviously, we have many right opinions which are true but not clear and distinct—but I only maintain that all that is clear and distinct is true.

SOCRATES: Perhaps we should again leave this "loose end" up to the reader to tie up. Using your definitions of clear and distinct, can he find any clear and distinct idea that is not true? For instance, could your hypothetical evil demon possibly put into his mind an idea that is so clear that he finds it psychologically impossible to keep it out, and reject it, and so distinct that it cannot be confused with anything else, but nevertheless this idea is false?

But for now, I would prefer to proceed to the rest of your system.

17

Step Five of Descartes' Philosophical System: Proofs for God's Existence

SOCRATES: So far you have proved the existence only of yourself as a thinking mind. You have not proved the existence of anything else.

DESCARTES: Correct.

SOCRATES: So you must build a bridge from the self to the other, whatever the other is. And if you fail to build the bridge—if you fail to prove the existence of anything besides yourself—you will end up in solipsism, the "ism" that claims all that exists is *sole ipse, only myself.*

DESCARTES: That is correct.

SOCRATES: Do you know what "only myself" is a definition of?

DESCARTES: You just said it, Socrates. That is a definition of solipsism, which I will overcome by my next proof.

SOCRATES: Yes, but if your next proof does not work, you will not overcome it. And perhaps it would be useful to contemplate just what that "it" is that you would not overcome—what the state of solipsism is a description of.

DESCARTES: I do not understand what you are suggesting.

SOCRATES: You are a Catholic, are you not?

DESCARTES: Yes.

SOCRATES: And a well-educated one. You have read your saints and mystics, have you not?

DESCARTES: Yes.

SOCRATES: Then you should know that according to some of your Catholic saints and mystics, that is the definition of Hell: pure egotism, pure loneliness, the total absence of the other. One of the mystics opines that there could not be physical fire in Hell because that would mean there was something else besides the damned soul, and that would relieve the gnawing of the ego on itself. She opined that physical pain could be a relief from spiritual pain. Another author added that that is why, when we are in deep despair, we induce physical pain in ourselves, by banging our head against the wall, or by tearing our hair out.

DESCARTES: Oh, Socrates, it is only a thought-experiment!

SOCRATES: I understand that. But it is a very serious one, is it not? Could there be a more serious one? Could there be a state more necessary to be saved from, even in thought?

DESCARTES: Not if it is Hell.

SOCRATES: Then we must attend to the building of your "bridge" from the self to the other with great care.

DESCARTES: I assure you, I have done exactly that in my thought. My bridge is strong, because God is that bridge. For of all the many ideas in my mind, I found only one, other than the idea of my own existence, that proved itself, so to speak; that was totally clear and distinct and indubitable, and that is the idea of God. I have not proved the existence of matter, or time, or space, or the world, so I cannot use premises taken from these sources to prove the existence of God. But the idea of God is unlike any other idea, such as the idea of a chain of causes, or the idea of design, which are questionable, and not self-evident; and the idea of God, clearly and distinctly defined, is the premise from which I prove the real existence of God, by showing that the existence of God is self-evident. So if solipsism is Hell, then God is my bridge out of Hell—and surely that is a secure and reliable bridge.

SOCRATES: In reality, certainly—if there is indeed a God. But in thought? That is what we must now question: have you proved that God exists? We must examine your proof.

DESCARTES: There are actually *two* proofs, or two versions of the proof, not just one. (There is a third, but it is very similar to one of the others, and the difference is so technical that we can omit it, if you don't mind.)

SOCRATES: Fine. Let us look at your two proofs one by one. The first is in the next paragraph:

DM 4, para. 4

Following this, reflecting upon the fact that I doubted and that, as a consequence, my being was not utterly perfect (for I saw clearly that it is a greater perfection to know than to doubt), I decided to search for the source from which I had learned to think of a thing more perfect than myself.

DESCARTES: "A thing more perfect than myself" is my first definition of God. A more perfect definition would be "a being that is totally perfect", but I do not need that definition in this first proof, as I will in my second proof. All I need here is the notion of a being more perfect than myself.

SOCRATES: That does not sound like "God" to me. A being more perfect than yourself could simply be a superior human mind, or an angel. How do you prove the existence of a being who deserves the name "God" from this imperfect notion?

DESCARTES: Because from this imperfect notion I go on, in the latter part of my proof, to the more perfect notion of a being "that had within itself all the perfections of which I could have any idea". Here is the passage:

DM 4, para. 4

. . . [A]nd I readily knew that this ought to originate from some nature that was in effect more perfect . . . for the receiving of this idea from nothing is a manifest impossibility; and since it is no less a contradic-

tion that something more perfect should follow from and depend upon something less
perfect, than that something can come from
nothing, I certainly could not obtain it from
myself. It thus remained that this idea was
placed in me by a nature truly more perfect
than I was, and even that *it had within itself all
the perfections of which I could have any idea;*
that is, to put my case in a single word, that
this nature was God.

You see, Socrates, my data and premise is simply
the idea of God in my mind. The idea occurs in my
mind, just as causes and effects occur in the physical
world. And whatever occurs, whether it is physical
or mental, must come either from nothing, or from
something. Since nothing can come from nothing, it
must come from something. Now there are two possibilities for that "something" let us call it the cause):
either it lacks, or it does not lack, some perfection
that is present in the thing that we have found to
occur (let us call it the effect). But if the cause lacks
that perfection, then that perfection arises in the effect without a cause. And that is just as impossible
as the *existence* of this thing-that-occurs arising from
nothing, from no cause at all. So the only cause adequate to account for the effect which is my idea of
God, is a real God that is at least as perfect as my
idea of God. Even if my idea of God is not *absolutely*
perfect, it is perfect enough to force me to ascribe
the title "God" to any being that corresponds to it.

SOCRATES: So your argument is that only a real God
can explain the occurrence of your idea of God.

DESCARTES: Yes.

SOCRATES: So if someone could adequately explain how your idea of God arose, without a real God, that would refute your proof.

DESCARTES: It would. But this is impossible, as I have shown. Nothing less perfect can cause something more perfect.

SOCRATES: What would you say to a thinker who claimed to explain the origin of the idea of God by wishful thinking? Surely all men deeply *wish* to be loved and cared for and guaranteed immortality. Why could our minds and hearts not invent the idea of God to compensate for our fear of loneliness and death?

DESCARTES: I have already answered that question, Socrates. Because our own minds and hearts, and our desire to be loved and immortalized, and our fear of loneliness and death, are all imperfect things. Thus they are all inadequate to account for any perfect effect. But my idea of God is the idea of something perfect, or more perfect, at least, than the sum total of all the things that are in me. Thus any possible psychological explanation, using only things that are in me, is inadequate to account for this perfect idea. As I say in my *Meditations*, explaining this principle of causality,

M 3,
para. 14

[I]t is evident by the light of nature [the nature of reason] **that at the very least there
must be as much in the total efficient cause
as there is in the effect of that same cause.
For, I ask, where can an effect get its real-**

**ity unless it be from its cause? And how can
the cause give that reality to the effect, unless the cause also has that reality?** [Nothing
can give what it does not have.] **Hence it follows that something cannot come into existence from nothing, nor even can what is
more perfect, that is, contains in itself more
reality, come into existence from what contains less. But this is clearly true not merely
for those effects whose reality is actual . . .
but also for ideas. . . .**

SOCRATES: I understand the logic of your argument.
But surely there are other cases, cases which do not
involve God, in which my mind, under the impress
of only very imperfect real things, invents something
that does not exist but which is much more perfect
than any of these real things. For instance, the idea
of a perfect saint, or an infallible philosopher.

DESCARTES: And how would *you* explain such ideas as
those, Socrates, without violating the logical principle that the more perfect cannot arise merely from
the less perfect?

SOCRATES: In this way. I would use your own principle of clear and distinct ideas, and distinguish two
clearly distinct realms, the realm of my mind and
the realm of the real world, or all the things outside
my mind, which might include matter, other minds,
and/or God. Let us call them the subjective realm
and the objective realm, or the subjective world and
the objective world. Within either one of these two
worlds, your principle holds: nothing more perfect

can arise from the less perfect. Greater ideas cannot come merely from lesser ideas, and greater things cannot come merely from lesser things. But suppose that one of these two worlds is greater than the other . . .

DESCARTES: That is exactly what I do suppose in my next proof for God's existence: that the objective world is greater than the subjective world; that it is more perfect to exist independent of my mind than to exist only as an idea dependent on my mind. And that is why I say that God must exist: because my idea of God is the idea of a being containing all perfections, and objective perfection is greater than merely subjective perfection.

SOCRATES: We will examine your second proof shortly. But since you do agree that one of these two worlds is greater than the other (since you say that to exist outside of or independent of your mind is more perfect than to exist as a mere idea in your mind), then it is not impossible that some set of imperfect causes from the more perfect objective world could bring about an effect in the subjective world that is more perfect than anything else in that subjective world, an idea that exceeds all other ideas. But it is still only an idea. I would rather have one imperfect but real wine, when I am thirsty, than a thousand perfect ideas of perfect wines.

DESCARTES: Ah, but the idea of God exists in *both* worlds, Socrates. Its *content*, or *meaning* is merely an idea—the idea of a perfect being. But its *occurrence* is a fact. A real person—myself, whose real existence

I have just proved, remember—really does have this idea. That is a fact that must be explained by other facts. And the God that explains it is a fact, not just an idea. No mere idea could cause a fact. No mere idea in the subjective realm could cause a fact to exist in the objective realm. So you must account for the fact that I do have this perfect idea of God even though I am an imperfect being.

To put the point more intuitively than logically, how could this mere clever ape have invented such an idea? Put all the ideas in the history of the world in one side of a scale, and put this single idea, the idea of God, in the other side, and weigh the two sides. On one side let there be Euclid's geometry, and the invention of fire, and the domestication of animals, and the laws of physics, and the subtleties of Scholastic philosophy, and all the great stories ever told by all the world's great storytellers. On the other side let there be simply this one idea of an infinitely perfect being, perfect in every way, all-powerful, all-knowing, all-wise, all-loving, all-good, all-just, all-beautiful. The one idea will infinitely outweigh all the other ideas, as infinity outweighs any finitude. Now this is certainly an impressive thing. Where could we imperfect creatures have gotten such an idea? We are like paupers carrying around a treasure in gold. Clearly it is a gift, and could have come only from a giver who is supremely rich. And this principle of causality—that every perfection in the effect must be present in the cause, or in the sum total of causes—surely this is as true in the world of ideas as it is in the world of bodily things.

SOCRATES: I think you have not yet answered my objection that something imperfect in the more perfect objective world could still cause something perfect in the less perfect subjective world. But let us leave that tricky question to the reader to pursue further, and let us explore your second proof for God's existence.

It is very similar to the most famous of all proofs for God's existence, in fact the most famous argument for anything in the history of philosophy, perhaps the most famous argument in all of human thought. It comes from St. Anselm, and would later be called the "ontological argument", the argument about God's *ontos* or being. Here is how you put it:

DM 4, para. 5

I saw very well that by supposing, for example, a triangle, it is necessary that its three angles be equal to two right angles; but I did not see anything in all this which would assure me that any triangle existed. On the other hand, returning to an examination of the idea I had of a perfect being, I found that existence was contained in it, in the same way as the fact that its three angles are equal to two right angles is contained in the idea of a triangle.

DESCARTES: Now there is an infallible proof for you!

SOCRATES: Why then is it one of the least convincing of all the arguments for God's existence? Only philosophers seem to take it seriously. If you ask anyone else for a good argument for God's existence, they will never give you this one, but some other, such as the chain of causes, or design, or the moral law, or miracles. They are always suspicious of this argument when they first hear it, and they feel as if you were performing a magic trick, pulling a live rabbit out of a dead hat, a real God out of a mere concept.

DESCARTES: I explained that defect in the popular mind in my very next paragraph:

> **But what makes many people become per-suaded that it is difficult to know this (i.e. the existence of the perfect being), and also even to know what kind of thing their soul is, is that they never lift their minds above sensible things and that they are so much in the habit of thinking about only what they can imagine (which is a particular way of thinking appropriate only for material things), that whatever is not imaginable seems to them to be unintelligible. This is obvious enough from what even the philosophers in the Schools take as a maxim: that there is nothing in the understanding that has not first been in the senses (where obviously the idea of God and the soul have never been).**

DM 4,
para. 6

SOCRATES: This brings us back to your criterion of truth, "clear and distinct ideas", which we have already examined, and, more generally, to your rationalism as contrasted to popular empiricism. But that is too large and diffuse an issue for us to examine profitably now. Perhaps it would be profitable for us some day to explore the answer the Scholastic philosophers, especially the Thomists, give to your challenge about the idea of God—an idea they admit is in the mind and has not been in the senses. How then can they say that there is nothing in the understanding that has not first been in the senses?

They do have an answer to this, and the answer centers on our ability to abstract intelligible forms and general principles from specific, concrete, material things and events that we sense. But although we have an infinity of time in this place, the readers on earth who will be reading this conversation do not, so we must make choices. And I choose that we now leave the investigation of this tangent also to ambitious readers, for I want to return to your second argument for God's existence.

It is hauntingly similar to your argument for your own existence. There, you argued that the proposition "I exist" is self-evident—because for you to deny your existence, you must exist—and here, you argue that the proposition "God exists" is self-evident —because real, objective existence is a perfection, and to deny God's existence is to affirm that God lacks this one perfection. And that is logically self-contradictory, for what both the believer, who affirms God's existence, and the unbeliever, who denies it, *mean* by "God" is "the being which by definition possesses *all* perfections, or all conceivable perfections". And real existence is one conceivable perfection. So atheism seems to be logically self-contradictory. For it maintains that "the being which, by definition, lacks no conceivable perfection, lacks this one conceivable perfection, namely objectively real existence."

DESCARTES: That is a very fine way of summarizing the argument, Socrates. Like my *cogito ergo sum*, it is not an argument with any questionable premises, because it has no premises at all. It is not so much a syllogism as a single self-evident proposition. You argued earlier, Socrates, that when I asserted that my own existence was self-evident, I was confusing myself with God, because I was assuming that existence was my very essence. Well, even if that criticism was just *there*—and I do not believe it was—it is certainly no criticism at all *here*. For God's essence *is* existence. That is why He needs no cause for His existence. So the very reason why you say my argument for my own existence did not work—that I am not God—is the reason why this argument does work—for God *is* God.

SOCRATES: Nevertheless, great philosophers have faulted this argument.

DESCARTES: Why?

SOCRATES: For no less than five reasons, I think.

DESCARTES: I am eager to hear and refute them.

SOCRATES: The first is from St. Thomas Aquinas. It is simply that we do not know God's essence, therefore we cannot use it as a term in this logical demonstration.

DESCARTES: I agree that we do not know God's essence. All I claim is that we can know that existence is part of it. And Aquinas affirms that too.

SOCRATES: Aquinas also argues, in the second place, that not everyone accepts this definition of God, as the being with all conceivable perfections. To such a person your argument would be worthless.

DESCARTES: Indeed. But such a person's mind is worthless. For this is the correct definition of God. If a fool defines God as a giant snake, I cannot be expected to tailor my argument to his false definition.

SOCRATES: Fair enough. But here is a third critique, also from Aquinas. It is essentially that you confuse concepts with judgments. The person who understands the meaning of the concept "God" must understand that all perfections are contained in it, and therefore that if existence is one of those perfections, then existence must also be contained in it. But . . .

DESCARTES: And that is exactly my argument.

SOCRATES: But perhaps "existence is not a perfection", as Immanuel Kant would argue later, in the nineteenth century, in criticizing Anselm's and your argument. This is essentially what Aquinas argued when he said that one who admitted that the concept of God contained the concept of existence did not thereby admit that the proposition "God exists" is true. For existence is not an essence, while all concepts are essences. Existence is affirmed or denied in a judgment, a proposition. It is not a subject or predicate term, but is the copula, the verb, the relation between the subject and predicate terms.

DESCARTES: That is a very technical, logical point. Shall we go into it here?

SOCRATES: No. Let us leave still another loose end to the reader. Instead, let us proceed to a fourth critique: that your argument confuses extension with comprehension. The class of "things that possess infinite perfection" may be an empty class. Just because we can define the content or comprehension of the class, that does not mean that there are any beings in the extension, the population, of the class.

DESCARTES: In other cases this is true. But not in the case of God. Here alone we can deduce extension from comprehension, existence from essence. We cannot argue that the most perfect conceivable philosopher really exists simply because existence is one conceivable perfection and a great philosopher who had this one perfection would be greater than a philosopher who lacked it. For "a philosopher" is not defined as "one who by definition has *all* conceivable perfections". Only God is that. So only God can be proved in this way.

SOCRATES: But this is another rather technical logical point. Let me proceed to a fifth criticism of your "ontological argument", which is perhaps the simplest criticism of all.

Your argument begins with the definition of the concept "God" as "the being which by definition contains all conceivable perfections", as the concept of a triangle contains by definition three angles equal to the sum of two right angles.

DESCARTES: That is correct.

SOCRATES: And the conclusion of your demonstration is that God exists, that God has real existence. For He has all perfections, and existence is a perfection (let us grant that, though Kant and Aquinas dispute it), therefore He has existence.

DESCARTES: That is as simple and certain a syllogism as you will find anywhere.

SOCRATES: And yet it seems to commit a logical fallacy.

DESCARTES: No way! "X has all Ys, and Z is a Y, therefore X has Z"—there is no fallacy there. Which of Aristotle's six rules of the syllogism do you say that argument violates?

SOCRATES: The first: that a syllogism must have only three terms. Yours has four. It commits "the fallacy of four terms".

DESCARTES: If you will count carefully, Socrates, you will see that there are only three. I realize you are old, and perhaps mathematics was not your forte, but . . .

SOCRATES: I assure you I can count, perhaps better than you can. For this God that you prove in your conclusion, this is the real God, and not just the idea of God, right?

DESCARTES: Right. I *assume* only the idea of God, not the real God. But I *prove* the real God, not just the idea of God. I prove the reality *from* the idea. If I had assumed the real God, I would be begging the question. And if I had proved only the idea of God, I would not be proving that God really exists.

SOCRATES: So this "God" in your conclusion is not just a concept but a reality.

DESCARTES: Yes.

SOCRATES: We put quotation marks around concepts, to show that we are treating them only as concepts. You would not put quotation marks around the word "God" in your conclusion, would you?

DESCARTES: No. As I said, if I had proved only the idea of God, or the concept of God, I would have proved nothing.

SOCRATES: Now the "God" you begin with, in your premise: Is that the real God?

DESCARTES: No. I do not begin with the real God, I end with the real God. As I said, if I began with the real God, I would be begging the question, assuming what I was supposed to prove.

SOCRATES: What do you begin with?

DESCARTES: The definition of God, admitted by atheist and theist alike.

SOCRATES: The concept of God, in other words.

DESCARTES: Yes.

SOCRATES: And we put quotation marks around a concept, do we not, to show that we are treating it merely as a concept, and not as a reality?

DESCARTES: Yes.

SOCRATES: Well, then, you have four terms: first, the concept of God, or "God" (in quotation marks), in the premise; second, existence; third, perfection; and fourth, the God without quotation marks, in the conclusion.

DESCARTES: Oh. Hmm . . . I think I can explain and defend myself here too, Socrates, though it will require a little knowledge of logic to follow my defense. . . .

SOCRATES: And once again I choose to press on, leaving this loose end also to the reader.

DESCARTES: As you please. I am obedient to your authority.

SOCRATES: And since my authority comes from above, your obedience bodes well for your eventual fate, once this purgatorial inquisition is finished. Let us then press on to your next point.

18

Step Six of Descartes' Philosophical System: The Proof of the Existence of the Material World

SOCRATES: This is a very short and simple point, but what it claims to prove is the whole world. Here you prove, finally, that the world we see with our senses exists. But you can do this only after you have proved that God exists, because God is the only premise that you can use to prove the world as your conclusion.

DESCARTES: Yes, that is my strategy. I know of no other way to prove the world's existence, once I have chosen to practice universal methodic doubt.

SOCRATES: What do you say to the criticism that is often given of your strategy here that it is exactly the opposite of the way the human mind does in fact always work? We begin by knowing things in the material world, at a very early age, because they seem the most obvious to us; then, later, we think about ourselves; and last of all we think about God, who seems the least obvious and the most questionable. But you end with the world rather than beginning with it, and you know God before the world rather than after it, and you know the world after you know the self rather than before it.

DESCARTES: I say that this is no criticism at all, for it misunderstands my enterprise. I am not a psychologist trying to account for the rise of these three different ideas in the mind of a typical growing child. I am a philosopher trying to prove the existence of self, God, and world. The critic simply is confusing the logical order with the psychological order.

SOCRATES: I think that is a clear and fair reply.

DESCARTES: So let us examine my proof of the world.

SOCRATES: It occurs, it seems to me, in three steps. First you prove the premise that God is all good, and therefore not a deceiver. Then you prove that if the world did not exist, God would be a deceiver. Then you draw your conclusion that the world exists.

DESCARTES: That is indeed my argument

SOCRATES: The first premise, then, is proved thus:

DM 4,
para. 4

[T]o know the nature of God, as far as my own nature was able, I had only to consider each thing about which I found an idea in myself, whether or not it was a perfection to have them, and I was certain that none of those that were marked by any imperfection were in this nature, but that all other perfections were.

DESCARTES: You see, I begin with the very same definition of God that I used in my proof of His existence: that God is the being that contains all conceivable perfections. I do not see how anyone could dispute that. And if I were systematically deceived simply by following the natural light of reason, that is, by using my mind according to its own innate rules, then God would be responsible for deceiving me.

SOCRATES: Why do you blame God for that?

DESCARTES: Because in following my innately and naturally known principles, I would be following His design, since He is the author of my being.

SOCRATES: But you have not proved that yet: that He is the author of your being.

DESCARTES: But no one denies that who accepts the existence of God. That idea is just as much a part of the essential meaning of the concept "God" as the idea that He contains all perfections.

SOCRATES: But your mind is imperfect, is it not? You made that point earlier: that you find doubts and errors in yourself, and therefore imperfections.

DESCARTES: True.

SOCRATES: If it is imperfect, might it not err in ascertaining just *how* imperfect it is? And also *when* it is in error?

DESCARTES: Of course.

SOCRATES: And what if your mind were so imperfect that by following what you call "the light of nature" you erred?

DESCARTES: As I said before, Socrates, in that case God would be a deceiver. Why do you go over this same argument once again?

SOCRATES: I want to explore this possibility, if you don't mind. Do you believe that your brain is the bodily instrument used by your mind, and that your brain is in some ways like a computer?

DESCARTES: A what?

SOCRATES: A calculating machine. Your contemporary Pascal invented the first one. It was basically an adding machine. But far more complex versions would be invented later. None of them would ever be quite as complex as the human brain. But the brain could be seen as a very complex thinking machine, or computer, although it is also much more than that.

DESCARTES: I understand that. But why do you bring up this analogy between the brain and a computer?

SOCRATES: Because someone has to invent and design and manufacture a computer, and to program it to do what it does. And if the human brain is like a computer, the same would apply to it: its activity (which is thinking) stems from its inner design and programs, what they will call, respectively, its "hardware" and its "software". That would seem to be a sound analogy, would it not?

DESCARTES: Let us grant that.

SOCRATES: Now what are the possibilities regarding the cause, or designer, or programmer of any machine, whether it is some other machine that is not a computer at all, or some other computer besides the human brain, or that computer which is the human brain? Could we not say that either this programmer is trustable or not?

DESCARTES: Necessarily so.

SOCRATES: And what would make it trustable?

DESCARTES: Two things, I think: it must be intelligent and it must be good, or beneficent, or nondeceptive. For if it lacked all intelligence, then the machine would be programmed by mere chance, and no one would trust such a machine. And if it had intelligence but not enough of it, and if it frequently made mistakes, then this machine that it programmed would be imperfectly programmed, and it would also make mistakes simply by following its own inner design. So it must be not only intelligent but totally intelligent, in fact infallible, if this machine that it designed is to be totally trustable.

The machine may still be misused, as we often misuse our intelligence. But as long as we do not misuse the machine, as long as we judge only according to its rules and its evidence, we do not err—if the machine itself is totally trustable. Thus, nothing less than the infallible God must be the cause of the thinking machine that is our brain, if we are to trust our thought at all, especially those naturally known principles of logic such as the law of noncontradiction that are so clear and distinct that we cannot doubt them.

SOCRATES: That is exactly what I thought you would say, and I must agree with you.

DESCARTES: But this God, or programming being, must be not only infallible and not able to be deceived, but also not able to deceive. He must be morally perfect, and that means beneficent. For I do not see how he could be excused from the moral imperfection of lying if he programmed our brains to deceive us. And this is a second quality of the being all men call God.

SOCRATES: I must agree with your reasoning here also, René.

DESCARTES: And therefore, if God is the source of our ability to think, and God does not deceive us, our thinking is correct as long as we do not violate its own natural and essential principles.

And it is as impossible for us to doubt the testimony of our senses as it is for us to doubt the testimony of our minds. So our senses also must be nondeceiving, as long as we do not misuse them and judge beyond the evidence they provide us.

SOCRATES: What do you mean by that last qualification?

DESCARTES: That the senses do not give us *judgments*, as the logic of thought does, but only *data*. For instance, we see a bright, round yellow disk in the sky, which we call the sun. We also see another round yellow disk in the sky, considerably less bright, which we call the moon. These two disks are so similar in apparent size that either one can eclipse the other. But for our mind to judge that they are in fact the same size is an example of judging beyond the evidence. For the moon is much closer to the earth than the sun, and so it *appears* as large as the sun whereas in fact it is much smaller. Another example: we see a stick in the water and it seems bent, though it is in fact straight. We may judge the stick to be really bent, but that is judging beyond the sensory evidence. Our senses do not deceive us. We see correctly, but we see the light from the stick refracted through the water.

SOCRATES: Once again, I cannot help but agreeing with what you say.

DESCARTES: Then we may accept the existence of the material world that our senses reveal to us, on the authority of God's trustability.

SOCRATES: If your arguments for God are correct.

DESCARTES: Of course.

SOCRATES: But those arguments began with the concept of God in your mind, and with the innately known principles of logic such as the law of causality: the principle that there can be no more in the effect than in the cause.

DESCARTES: Yes, and we can know that these principles are true because our mind has been programmed by a trustable God.

SOCRATES: If instead we had been programmed by the evil demon, or by blind chance, we would have no reason to trust these innate principles, isn't that so?

DESCARTES: Yes, indeed.

SOCRATES: And how do we know that this is not the case?

DESCARTES: By my arguments for God.

SOCRATES: But those arguments began by assuming these innate principles.

DESCARTES: Oh.

SOCRATES: So you have proved the existence and trustability of God by the natural and innate principles of logic with which all human minds have been programmed, and you have proved the trustability of these principles of logic by the existence and trustability of God. Again you seem to be arguing in a circle.

DESCARTES: I think I can escape this circle, Socrates, for these principles do not formally and logically presuppose the existence of God. Atheists too know them. It is self-contradictory to deny them. In objective fact, God is the source of these principles, but in our subjective knowledge, the principles are the source of our knowledge of God. By distinguishing these two worlds, the objective world and the subjective world of thought, I avoid the circle. God is in fact the absolutely first, and these principles are in thought the absolutely first.

SOCRATES: But the only way you can prove God is to assume the validity of these principles. And the only way you can prove the validity of these principles is to demonstrate them from the premise that there is a trustable God, who is their author. So you do still seem to argue in a circle.

DESCARTES: Then I will demonstrate these principles without the use of God as a premise, I will do it as Aristotle did. I will show that it is self-contradictory to deny them.

SOCRATES: But suppose the law of noncontradiction itself is not true? Suppose you are systematically deceived into thinking it is true by some evil demon who designed your mind to err and not to know it errs, and not to be able even to conceive the possibility that it errs when it follows these laws?

DESCARTES: A fantastic hypothesis, Socrates.

SOCRATES: Indeed, but it is your own hypothesis, René, which flowed from the first step of your method, universal doubt. Remember?

DESCARTES: Do you think that the only way to demonstrate these principles is to assume the existence of God?

SOCRATES: No, I do not say that.

DESCARTES: Then if we can demonstrate them in some other way, we can escape the circle. And we can do this in Aristotle's indirect way, when he refuted the skepticism of Protagoras and the Sophists in his *Metaphysics*. We can demonstrate the truth of such self-evident principles indirectly, even though we cannot demonstrate them directly by deducing them from principles that are more basic than they, for they are the most basic principles of all. And this indirect demonstration consists in showing that anyone who denies these principles, such as noncontradiction and causality, really affirms them, as we do. For if he denies the law of noncontradiction, which affirms that contradictory propositions cannot both be true, he affirms that contradictories *can* both be true; and the contradictory of noncontradiction is contradiction; and thus the denier of the law of noncontradiction is really saying that contradiction equals noncontradiction. So his law of contradiction, the law that he says he believes in instead of the law of noncontradiction that we believe in, turns out to be its opposite, its contradictory. So he too believes in noncontradiction. To deny the law of noncontradiction is to affirm it.

SOCRATES: That is a very clever demonstration, René, but what if the principles you used in it are also part of the evil demon's deception? As your critic Pascal noted, when speaking of these innately known logical principles,

> We cannot be sure that these principles are true (faith and revelation apart) except through some natural intuition. Now this natural intuition affords no convincing proof that they are true. There is no certainty, apart from faith, as to whether man was created by a good God, an evil demon, or just by chance. And so it is a matter of doubt, depending on our origin, whether these innate principles are true, false, or uncertain. (*Pensées* 131)

DESCARTES: I am astonished to have been brought to this point. You and Pascal both seem to be more the doubters than I, Socrates.

SOCRATES: Ah, the secret is out at last!

DESCARTES: I never would have believed that I could be brought to admit what I have just admitted.

SOCRATES: Only because you doubted so little, did it take you this long to realize how little you doubted.

19

Descartes and the Future of Mankind

SOCRATES: Our last two sections can be taken together, I think, for the fifth part of your *Discourse* is not about philosophy at all but about the physical sciences, which do not directly concern us here, except as they affect your point in the sixth part, where you predict the consequences if mankind adopts your method in the sciences.

DESCARTES: Fair enough.

SOCRATES: And this one longish passage at the beginning of Part Six seems to sum up your ultimate promise, your salesman's pitch, so to speak. First, you speak of the importance of your contribution to the physical sciences:

. . . [A]s soon as I had acquired some general notions in the area of physics, and, beginning to test them on various specific difficulties, I had noticed just how far they can lead and how much they differ from the principles that people have used up until the present, I believed I could not keep them hidden away without greatly sinning against the law that

DM 6, para. 2

obliges us to procure as best we can the common good of all men. . . .

DESCARTES: I always saw myself as a scientist first rather than a philosopher, Socrates.

SOCRATES: I understand that. What strikes me in this passage is a single word, a very serious word and one that you have never used before—apparently indicating that all the things you said before were less serious, less important, than this.

DESCARTES: What word is that, Socrates?

SOCRATES: The word "sinning". You seem to see the sin against the future physical improvement of the lot of mankind on earth as the greatest sin, or at least the only one that deserves mention. The only other thing you said in this book about morals was your wholly provisional and pragmatic code in Part Three.

DESCARTES: When you see some of the consequences of the use of my new method, you will understand why I take this so seriously, Socrates.

SOCRATES: Then let us do just that. You say:

DM 6,
para. 2

For these general notions show me that it is possible to arrive at knowledge that is very useful in life and that in place of the speculative philosophy taught in the Schools, one can find a practical one, by which, knowing the force and the actions of fire, water, air, stars, the heavens, and all the other bodies that surround us, just as we understand the various skills of our craftsmen, we could, in the same way, use these objects for all the

purposes for which they are appropriate, and thus make ourselves, as it were, masters and possessors of nature.

Here you show your kinship with Francis Bacon. In fact you use almost the very same expression he does: "man's conquest of nature".

DESCARTES: Our epistemologies and our methods are opposites, though, for he is an Empiricist and I am a Rationalist.

SOCRATES: But your end is the same, and the kinship of ends is deeper than the kinship of means, because ends are chosen by the heart, while means are chosen by the head.

DESCARTES: Yes, that is so.

SOCRATES: Then this is by far the most radical and the most important part of your book, for it is not only about the ultimate end of your philosophy, but about the ultimate end of human life on earth. A new ultimate end, or greatest good, or *summum bonum*— how could there possibly be a more radical change than that?

DESCARTES: But men have always longed to conquer nature, pain, ignorance, suffering, and death. I merely give them the new means to this perennial end. What is radical in my thought is simply that it works. So I subtract nothing, I only add something.

SOCRATES: I do not see that. Rather, I see something else in your book, something much more radical, and it seems to be not merely an addition but a subtraction, or at least a replacement.

DESCARTES: Where do you see this?

SOCRATES: In the passage I just quoted, where you say that *"in place of* the speculative philosophy taught in the Schools, one can find a practical one." So it is not merely a question of a *more* practical one replacing a *less* practical one, but of practical philosophy replacing speculative philosophy.

DESCARTES: And I stand by that, when it comes to the sciences. I do not mean to apply it to theology, or to deny the value of the contemplative life there. After all, God is not given to us to be used but to be known and loved. But this world, according to God's own Holy Book, was given to us as a garden to be tilled and worked on, that is, to be used. I think my practical attitude is the right one when it comes to the natural sciences. And this is exactly what Bacon called for too.

SOCRATES: But Bacon also criticized the classical idea, taught in the Schools both of ancient Greece and of medieval Christendom, that knowledge—knowledge as such, knowledge of anything—is an end to be pursued for its own sake. That is why they called it "speculative" science—not because it was uncertain, but because it sought simply to see, to contemplate, to look, to know, for its own sake. (As you know, a *speculum* in Latin means a "looking-glass", a mirror.)

But Bacon said, instead, that knowledge should not be sought as an end in itself but as a means to the higher end of power over nature. "Knowledge is *power*" was his slogan. I wonder whether you agree with him.

DESCARTES: I certainly agree that knowledge *is* power. "The pen is mightier than the sword." And I think you do not deny that either.

SOCRATES: But that is not the question. The question is about ends. Is knowledge a means and power the end? Of the two terms in Bacon's slogan, clearly it is power that is for him the end and knowledge that is merely the means. And this is truly radical, for it is a radical reordering of ultimate ends.

DESCARTES: How so? Could you explain that more clearly?

SOCRATES: I think so. Old Aristotle had taught, and all Christendom had believed, that power was not the highest thing, and that therefore the kind of knowledge that issues in power over nature, which Aristotle called *techne* or "know-how" and which later ages will call "technology", is not the most valuable kind of knowledge.

DESCARTES: I would agree that it is secondary in value, but still very great.

SOCRATES: For Aristotle it was not even secondary; it was tertiary. It was only the *third* most valuable kind of knowledge.

DESCARTES: Only third?

SOCRATES: Yes indeed. For much more important than this was what he called "practical knowledge", by which he meant not technology but something like moral knowledge, knowledge of how to live better, how to act, how to "practice" the art of living, both individually and in the household and in the state.

This is the knowledge you claimed to seek when you complained that the ancients had based their knowledge of the virtues on an uncertain foundation, and you proposed a securer foundation for this kind of knowledge.

DESCARTES: And I reaffirm that the knowledge of how to live virtuously is even more important than the knowledge of the conquest of nature. For as I said in one of my moral maxims, we should conquer ourselves first, and nature second. For we always have power over ourselves and our choices, and even over our passions, by the cultivation of virtue, but we do not always have power over nature. Certainly, at the point of death we lose our power over nature.

SOCRATES: That was the promise you left us in Part Three. But you never fulfilled your promise. All you gave us was a purely provisional code of morals that had no sense of obligation or necessity in it, a code designed for nothing but maximum peace and comfort while you were finishing up the work you obviously thought much more important: your system of philosophy and the sciences.

DESCARTES: I have an excuse for that, Socrates. It is called death, the thing that is the least under our power. I was not given the time to fulfill my promise.

SOCRATES: Did you not know that any man could die at any moment?

DESCARTES: Of course.

SOCRATES: Then why did you not spend the uncertain amount of time you had in the more important

DESCARTES AND THE FUTURE OF MANKIND   225

sciences of morality rather than in the less important sciences of natural science and technology?

DESCARTES: Because that was where my God-given talents lay. And because many others had already written excellent treatises on morality, men both wiser and more moral than myself.

SOCRATES: That answer also seems reasonable. But my point is not about what Aristotle called the practical sciences, the moral sciences, but about what he called the speculative sciences. For even moral knowledge was only second in importance and value to Aristotle. He ranked the knowledge of the truth for its own sake above even the knowledge of the truth for the sake of putting it into practice in your life.

DESCARTES: Very foolishly, in my opinion.

SOCRATES: Do you know his reasons, so that you can argue against them?

DESCARTES: It was simply a prejudice of his age and of his pride in what he and his culture did best, which was this purely speculative knowledge.

SOCRATES: That is not true. He gave a reason.

DESCARTES: And what was it?

SOCRATES: The very same reason that justified ranking moral knowledge over technological knowledge was the reason that justified ranking speculative knowledge over moral knowledge.

DESCARTES: And what reason was that?

SOCRATES: The value of the thing the knowledge perfected, or improved.

DESCARTES: What do you mean?

SOCRATES: Technological knowledge perfects material things in nature that we use: things like water
wheels, ships, or cooking stoves. Moral knowledge
perfects something much more important and much
more intimate to us, more close to home, so to speak,
namely, our very actions, our lives. That is why it is
more important than technology: because our lives
are more important than the lives of ships or pots.

DESCARTES: I do not deny that.

SOCRATES: But that very same reason explains why
speculative knowledge is the most important of all:
because the thing it perfects is even more intimate,
more valuable, more close to our essence, than the
thing moral knowledge perfects.

DESCARTES: What could be even closer to our essence
than our lives?

SOCRATES: Our essence itself—which you yourself
locate in thought. Speculative knowledge perfects our
mind, enlarges the mind, which is even more intimate
and interior than our actions.

DESCARTES: I see the wisdom in that and do not deny
it. I think there must be a way to hold both ideals,
the old and the new, without contradiction. And even
a way of holding both *rankings*, the ancient ranking
of the speculative over the practical and the modern
ranking of the practical over the speculative. Though
that seems contradictory, we can make a distinction
that overcomes the contradiction, a distinction of

different dimensions, or different points of view, or something like that.

SOCRATES: Perhaps so. Again I will choose to leave that question to the reader, so that we can proceed to the very next thing you say in this paragraph of prophecy. For it seems radical indeed. Here is how far you hope to go with your new knowledge of nature:

This is desirable not only for the invention of an infinity of devices that would enable us to enjoy without pain the fruits of the earth and all the goods one finds in it [thus reversing one of the consequences of Adam's fall, "in the sweat of your brow shall you eat bread"], **but also principally for the maintenance of health, which unquestionably is the first good and the foundation of all the other goods in this life.**

DM 6, para. 2

I note that you are the first philosopher in history to choose health as your candidate for the *summum bonum*. A strange candidate for a young man in a new, young age; for that is the answer the old give when asked for their highest value: "If you have your health, you have everything." Have you ever heard a healthy young man say that?

DESCARTES: But I give my reason for it in the next sentence. Read on, please.

SOCRATES: I shall.

For even the mind depends so greatly upon the temperament and on the disposition of

the organs of the body that, were it possible to find some means to make men generally more wise and competent than they have
been up until now, I believe that one should
look to medicine to find this means.

DESCARTES: By medicine I did not mean merely the
restoration of health to bodies that were ill, but the
improvement of the bodily health of all men, of every
age and condition. As I go on to explain:

It is true that medicine currently practiced
contains little of such usefulness; but without trying to ridicule it, I am sure that there
is no one, not even among those in the medical profession who would not admit that everything we know is almost nothing in com-
parison to what remains to be known, and
that we might rid ourselves of an infinity of
maladies, both of body and mind, and even
perhaps also the enfeeblement brought on by
old age, were one to have a sufficient knowledge of their causes and of all the remedies
that nature has provided us.

SOCRATES: Are you suggesting . . .

DESCARTES: I do not suggest it. I state it. There is
no reason in principle why a perfected science cannot discover a perfected health and cure every known
disease.

SOCRATES: Even old age?

DESCARTES: Even old age.

SOCRATES: But if we never die of disease, and we never die of old age, and we are not killed in war or by assassination, we become immortal. Is that what you suggest here?

DESCARTES: Burman once asked me such a question. And this is what I answered him in 1648, in Amsterdam:

Whether man was immortal before the Fall, and if so how, is not a question for the philosopher, but must be left to the theologians. And as to how men before the Flood could achieve such an advanced age, this is something which defeats the philosopher; and it may be that God brought this about miraculously, by means of supernatural causes, and without recourse to physical causes. Or then again, it could have been that the structure of the natural world was different before the Flood, and that it then deteriorated as a result of the Flood. The philosopher studies nature, as he does man, simply as it is now; he does not investigate its causes at any more profound level, since this is beyond him. However, it should not be doubted that human life could be prolonged, if we knew the appropriate art. For since our knowledge of the appropriate art enables us to increase and prolong the life of plants and such like, why should it not be the same with man? (Conversations with Burman, Amsterdam, April 20, 1648)

This is why I wrote, in the very last paragraph of my *Discourse on Method*, that

I have resolved to spend my remaining lifetime only in trying to acquire a knowledge of nature which is such that one could deduce from it rules for medicine that are more certain than those in use at present.

SOCRATES: Well, you were not given enough time, were you?

DESCARTES: No, but can you tell me about the success of my successors?

SOCRATES: I can tell you this much: that the average human lifetime was indeed increased in the centuries that followed your death.

DESCARTES: How much?

SOCRATES: In the nations that had the scientific, technological, and medical knowledge, it reached threescore and ten by the time three centuries had passed.

DESCARTES: That is not very much. In fact, that is the length of life that the Bible states is appointed to man back in King David's time. Was medicine not improved much?

SOCRATES: Oh, very much.

DESCARTES: And were cures not found for many diseases?

SOCRATES: They were. But for every new cure, there seemed to be a new disease.

DESCARTES: Did mankind not use my method to advance the science of medicine?

SOCRATES: No, because your method proved worthless there. They found that only induction, not deduction, could discover the rules of medicine and the causes and cures of diseases.

DESCARTES: Hmm. But mankind did make great progress in medicine.

SOCRATES: It was probably the single most beneficial result of the new science.

DESCARTES: I am gratified to know that. But . . . I hesitate to ask . . .

SOCRATES: Out with it! There is no hiding here.

DESCARTES: Did no one suggest anything more?

SOCRATES: You mean the conquest of death itself, nature's trump card?

DESCARTES: Well, that would be the supreme triumph of "man's conquest of nature", would it not?

SOCRATES: Indeed it would. And nearly four hundred years after you wrote this book, the dream began to rise again from its grave.

DESCARTES: Why do you use such a ghastly image?

SOCRATES: I will tell you outright, without any cross-examination: because it is a ghastly idea. It is, in fact, an idea that, if it were implemented, would be the single most disastrous idea in the entire history of the world since the idea to eat the forbidden fruit. In a sense, it is the same idea: the idea of sneaking past the angel's flaming sword, back into Eden, to eat the fruit of the tree of life and immortalizing the state mankind fell into by eating the fruit of the other tree, the forbidden one.

DESCARTES: Why is that such a disastrous idea? Because it is impossible?

SOCRATES: No, because it is possible.

DESCARTES: But that would be paradise on earth.

SOCRATES: No, it would be Hell on earth.

DESCARTES: I am appalled and astounded to hear that. I do not understand.

SOCRATES: Have you ever smelled an egg that never hatched?

DESCARTES: I have indeed.

SOCRATES: Then you have smelled the world you hoped for.

DESCARTES: You mean we are *designed* to "hatch", to die and resurrect.

SOCRATES: Yes.

DESCARTES: So a world without hatchers would be a world of rotten eggs.

SOCRATES: Exactly. But the grace of God, which gave you your remarkable intelligence, by which you discovered your new method, and many other great discoveries in the sciences, also gave you the gift of an early death, so that you did not have the time to create that world of rotten eggs, or to live in it.

DESCARTES: It seems I have some deeper and more mysterious learning to do than this logical examination of the philosophical ideas in my book on method!

SOCRATES: And because you are open to that correction, it shall be graciously given to you. Pray that it also be given to the fools who now pursue your dark dream on earth.

20

Descartes' Legacy

DESCARTES: Was I then too naïve and optimistic about human nature and the use of power?

SOCRATES: Yes. But you had a good motive and a good excuse. You saw the horrible effects of the Thirty Years' War, and you hoped you could help the world to peace through your reliance on reason. Indeed, this was one of the noblest goals of the movement you are usually credited with fathering, a movement that called itself the "Enlightenment".

DESCARTES: And did it succeed?

SOCRATES: It did not. In fact, in the twentieth century more men were murdered for political reasons, both in and out of declared wars, than the sum total of the entire population of the world in my day.

DESCARTES: I am totally at a loss. This is certainly not what either Bacon or I had in mind when we spoke of "man's conquest of nature". It seems to have resulted only in man's conquest of other men using nature as their instruments.

SOCRATES: That is exactly what a prophetic philosopher named C. S. Lewis said three centuries after your death. His book was entitled *The Abolition of*

Man. But look here! We are no longer alone. We have a guest. And I think you recognize him.

DESCARTES: Pascal! You who called my philosophy "useless and uncertain". Are you here to taunt me?

PASCAL: No, I am here to finish what Socrates began in questioning you so that you may better know yourself.

DESCARTES: Apparently I have a lot to learn from both of you—but Socrates has already disappeared. Our conversation was by no means completed.

PASCAL: He will return, I guarantee you. Very often.

DESCARTES: Well, if it is you who will now play the part of Socrates to me, what questions would you like me to answer?

PASCAL: I would like to know what kind of benefits you hoped your method, and its applications in science and technology, would give to the world. Could you give me some specific examples?

DESCARTES: Why do you want to know that?

PASCAL: So that we can evaluate your hopes by the standard of history.

DESCARTES: Fair enough. Well, I hoped for such things as this: that future generations would be able to travel quickly and easily around the world in great machines, rocket ships, in just a few hours; and that they would be able to cook meat in efficient ovens in just a few minutes with inexpensive fuels like natural gas. For in my day it took half a year to travel around the world and half a day to cook a meal.

PASCAL: I will tell you, then, that such rocket ships did exist, three centuries after you, and such ovens too. But I must add that the rocket ships were used to carry, not passengers, but bombs that were so powerful that a single one could destroy a whole city. And I must add that these efficient and inexpensive gas ovens of yours were indeed invented, but I must add that the most educated, scientific, and technological nation on earth would use them to cook six million innocent human beings in them.

DESCARTES: I am appalled and astounded. But I know you cannot lie here. I am simply sick when I contemplate this.

PASCAL: That is the one thing you failed to see, René: that you are sick, that all humanity is sick. Our theology called it "Original Sin"—did you think this was some arcane and worthless formula of the Schools?

DESCARTES: Was my philosophy wrong from the very beginning?

PASCAL: It was. For your starting point was your wisdom and end was your happiness. Your wisdom was your new method and the certainties you claimed it could prove, and your happiness was your hoped-for goal of the conquest of nature. Socrates has shown you the problems with your wisdom, and I have shown you the problems with your hope for happiness.

DESCARTES: And your philosophy, Pascal, what is its starting point?

PASCAL: A far more secure one, René. Its starting point was not "I am wise and happy" but "I am ignorant and unhappy, though I desire to be wise and happy." That is the fundamental data that must test every hypothesis. If we are to be true to life, we must try to find a philosophy that can best explain *those* four truths: that all men seek happiness; that none find it, that no one is truly happy in this world; that all men seek wisdom and certainty; and that none find it in this world. And as Socrates discovered, the more foolish they are, the more they believe they are wise.

DESCARTES: Where could such a pessimistic starting point ever lead you?

PASCAL: Come and see. Take and read my *Pensées*.